Genre-Based Strategies to Promote Critical Literacy in Grades 4–8

Genre-Based Strategies to Promote Critical Literacy in Grades 4–8

Danielle E. Hartsfield and Sue C. Kimmel

LIBRARIES
UNLIMITED®

An Imprint of ABC-CLIO, LLC

Santa Barbara, California • Denver, Colorado

Copyright © 2020 by Danielle E. Hartsfield and Sue C. Kimmel

All rights reserved. No part of this publication may be reproduced, stored in a retrieval system, or transmitted, in any form or by any means, electronic, mechanical, photocopying, recording, or otherwise, except for the inclusion of brief quotations in a review, without prior permission in writing from the publisher.

Library of Congress Cataloging in Publication Control Number: 2019029994

ISBN: 978-1-4408-6316-5 (paperback)
     978-1-4408-6317-2 (ebook)

24 23 22 21 20   1 2 3 4 5

This book is also available as an eBook.

Libraries Unlimited
An Imprint of ABC-CLIO, LLC

ABC-CLIO, LLC
147 Castilian Drive
Santa Barbara, California 93117
www.abc-clio.com

This book is printed on acid-free paper ∞

Manufactured in the United States of America

Contents

Introduction

Teaching students how to read from a critical literacy stance is a timely and relevant practice in a world where text is available at the swipe of a finger. To be critically literate readers and thinkers, students must learn to question what they read, asking themselves who wrote the text, why the text was written, and how the text positions themselves and others. *Genre-Based Strategies to Promote Critical Literacy in Grades 4–8* provides strategies and resources to school librarians and teachers interested in engaging middle-grade students in reading children's literature through a critical literacy lens.

Genre-Based Strategies to Promote Critical Literacy in Grades 4–8 is for anyone with an interest in contemporary children's literature and critical literacy, but it is particularly useful for school librarians and educators. In many cases, preparation programs for school librarians and teachers do not teach candidates how to incorporate critical literacy practices in library and classroom settings. *Genre-Based Strategies to Promote Critical Literacy in Grades 4–8* equips library and teacher candidates with practical, research-based ideas for enacting critical literacy practices in middle-grade libraries and classrooms. Chapters include information about children's literature genres and contemporary titles, and the book may serve as a supplemental or primary text for university courses in children's literature, literacy education, or language arts methods. In addition, *Genre-Based Strategies to Promote Critical Literacy in Grades 4–8* can be a resource for practicing librarians and educators who are seeking an introduction to critical literacy or searching for ideas to integrate critical literacy in their teaching. The strategies presented in this book can inspire, enrich, and enliven instruction.

This book is built on the premise that different genres demand a different mindset from readers. For example, when reading contemporary realistic fiction from a critical literacy stance, readers should consider how authors shape the readers' understanding of contemporary life by analyzing which social issues are at the forefront and which groups of people are privileged and marginalized in the text. Meanwhile, reading a nonfiction book about history demands that critically literate readers unpack the motivations behind why certain events are given prominence and which events may have been omitted. In *Genre-Based Strategies to Promote Critical Literacy in Grades 4–8*, we select titles from different genres and discuss how students can learn to analyze them from a critical literacy perspective. We share a variety of strategies for reading children's literature from a critical literacy perspective.

STRUCTURE OF THE BOOK

Genre-Based Strategies to Promote Critical Literacy in Grades 4–8 is written in a series of paired chapters. One chapter is devoted to explaining a particular genre or form of children's literature, and a following chapter provides a sample lesson plan modeling the application of a critical literacy strategy in a classroom or library. Even-numbered chapters are about genres and forms, while odd-numbered chapters include lesson plans (with the exception of Chapter 1). The following genres of children's literature are included: informational books (Chapter 2), narrative nonfiction and biographies (Chapter 4), historical fiction (Chapter 6), contemporary realistic fiction (Chapter 8), and fantasy (Chapter 10). We also discuss two special forms of children's literature: picture books (Chapter 12) and graphic novels (Chapter 14). These genres and forms do overlap; for example, a fantasy may be represented in a picture book or a graphic novel. However, picture book and graphic novel chapters are included because they merit their own treatment. With the inclusion of both images and written texts, these forms offer a unique opportunity to address multimodal literacies that are relevant to today's digital landscape. In addition, these forms invite readers to consider design decisions such as framing and page turns.

Each even-numbered chapter defines the genre or form, explains how to evaluate the notable characteristics of the genre or form, and discusses how each genre or form can be effectively read from a critical literacy stance by providing examples from contemporary children's titles. The information in these chapters can be useful to preservice librarians and teachers who are beginning to learn about different genres. It can also be beneficial to in-service librarians and teachers who want to deepen their knowledge of genre and become familiar with contemporary titles. For all readers, these chapters will demonstrate the thought processes behind reading a given genre or form from a critical literacy stance.

Moreover, each of these chapters features an annotated bibliography of fifteen to twenty titles that are recommended for critical analysis with middle-grade students. Titles chosen for inclusion were published in 2014 or later (within five years of this book's publication). To compile these bibliographies, annual lists of awards and best books were scanned for potential titles meeting the dual criteria of (1) quality literature, including writing, illustrations, and presentation; and (2) potential to engage students as critically literate readers. To meet this latter criterion, books addressing social issues (contemporary and historic) were given special consideration for inclusion. Some of these social issues include bullying, gender, disability, and cultural difference and inclusion. Some titles explicitly address a social issue, while others require more inference. For example, *George* deals directly with gender identity, while in *Wolf in the Snow*, social and cultural meanings can be interpreted through discussion of the visual presentation of the story. Though the majority of books included in the bibliography are highly recommended, on occasion, a title with serious flaws is included because it opens opportunities for critical literacy. As an example, Raina Telgemeier's *Ghosts* is included because the author's appropriation of another culture's practice and beliefs can invite conversations about power, cultural relationships, and who should be "allowed" to tell a culture's story.

Alternating chapters of the book explain critical literacy strategies that can be used with each genre. These odd-numbered "strategy chapters" include standards-aligned lesson plans adaptable to students in the middle grades. For example, a strategy chapter about creating multimodal text sets (Chapter 3) follows the genre chapter about informational books (Chapter 2). Chapter 3 explains how multimodal text sets can expose the subjectivity of facts by inviting readers to understand that all texts, even factual ones, reflect an author's choices of what information to include and exclude. These strategy chapters are beneficial to all readers and can be applied to a variety of titles and contexts. They can help pre-service librarians and teachers to plan future instruction and provide in-service librarians and teachers with practical ideas they can readily implement in their programming or teaching.

Each strategy chapter features one or two focus texts. These focus texts help explain the strategy and are included in the accompanying lesson plan. All of the focus texts included in the strategy chapters incorporate contemporary or historic social issues. This helps readers understand that being critically literate means making connections to real-world problems and social justice issues. For example, Kate Messner's chapter book *Breakout* is the focus text for the strategy chapter (Chapter 9) paired with the genre chapter on contemporary realistic fiction (Chapter 8). The protagonists of *Breakout* experience problems relatable to all children, such as fitting in and navigating friendships, but they also tackle issues of racial equality and discrimination. While strategies have been selected to match focus texts representing the featured genre, they may be used with other genres and texts. Readers are encouraged to skim these strategy chapters for ideas they might apply to other texts they have selected.

USING THE LESSON PLANS

The lessons in the lesson plans are generally presented for whole class use, but they are adaptable to small groups in a book club or other educational setting where smaller groups of students may be reading different texts. Most of the lessons require each student to have a copy of the book. In some cases, a book may be read aloud, particularly the shorter picture books, but access to multiple copies of the book for close examination is often desirable. Graphic novels particularly demand close examination of each page, and a copy is needed for every student or pair of students.

Critical literacy benefits from a diversity of reader perspectives. Grouping students in pairs or small groups allows for in-depth explorations and demands full participation of all members. In these cases, heterogeneous groupings of students may allow for more diverse perspectives. On the other hand, grouping students into larger configurations to share a text, including whole class, whole grade level, or whole school, opens possibilities for sharing of more perspectives. Educators might also consider partnering with another school or inviting parents or community members to share their perspectives on a topic or issue. This would further enhance a critical perspective regarding a text.

Often, a critical perspective asks the reader to go outside the text either to gather background information for a fuller understanding or to apply critical literacy strategies in other venues such as messages in the news media, political rhetoric, or advertising. For example, controversy regarding the graphic novel *Ghosts* might be best understood by reading or hearing from a Latinx perspective about the meaning of "Day of the Dead"—*Día de los Muertos*. Or in the case of visual images, students might apply strategies gained from studying picture books to examine visual messaging in advertising. A critical perspective asks readers to always push the boundaries of what they know and believe, and this benefits from perspectives outside oneself. Questions such as "How might I be wrong?" or "How might someone from another culture view this differently?" are important to a critical perspective. The school librarian serves in a key role to suggest resources that offer different perspectives or help to inform a broader understanding of a text.

A critical perspective may also call the reader to go outside the text and outside the classroom to take action in communities toward social justice. For example, learning about contemporary racial inequalities through reading and discussing *Breakout* could prompt students to ask questions about how discrimination manifests in their own communities. Students could devise a plan for calling attention to this issue and working toward ameliorating it. Readers of *Genre-Based Strategies to Promote Critical Literacy in Grades 4–8* are invited and encouraged to imagine ways they can extend the learning opportunities shared in these lesson plans according to their students' interests and the classroom and community context.

LESSON PLAN FORMAT

Each of the lesson plans in the strategy chapters includes step-by-step instructions for implementation and dialogue that educators might initiate with students. These lesson plans are not meant to be prescriptive; librarians and teachers can make adjustments based on their personal preferences and the needs of their students. However, the level of detail included in the lesson plans is necessary for two reasons: First, these details help readers visualize the lesson and clarify their understanding of how the lesson might proceed. Second, some readers of this book may be preservice teacher or library candidates. Exposure to detailed lesson plans like the ones in this book can help these candidates understand the amount of thought and intention required for a successful lesson.

For the sake of consistency, each lesson plan follows the same format. Here, we explain the elements of the lesson plan format to support readers' understanding.

Central focus: This is a statement summarizing the main idea of the lesson. It is written in third person and explains what students will accomplish in the lesson. The verb used in the central focus is the same verb that has been specified as the academic language function (see the following pages).

Subject: This refers to the content area(s) addressed in the lesson. All of the lesson plans in this book are linked to English language arts, but some lesson plans integrate content from other subjects (e.g., social studies as in the lesson plan featured in Chapter 5).

Grade: This is the grade level for which the lesson plan is intended. At least one lesson plan is included for each of the middle grades (4–8). However, the lesson plans are adaptable to various grade levels. Following each lesson plan, we discuss modifications that could make the lesson applicable to children at higher- or lower-grade levels.

Classroom context: This refers to whether the lesson plan is intended for the whole class or a small group.

Standards: Standards are intended educational outcomes determined by a state's governing body (e.g., the Georgia Department of Education). For the purpose of this book, we have included standards from the Common Core State Standards for English Language Arts (National Governors Association Center for Best Practices & Council of Chief State School Officers, 2010) because they have been adopted by the majority of states in the United States.

Objectives: Like standards, objectives are also intended educational outcomes. However, objectives are determined by teachers based on standards, and they are often written for a single lesson or unit of instruction. The lesson plans in this book apply the KUD format, meaning they explain what students should *know*, *understand*, or be able to *do* as a result of the lesson (Estes & Mintz, 2016). *Know* objectives convey the facts, definitions, or procedural knowledge that students should acquire as a result of the lesson. *Understand* objectives communicate "big ideas" or essential understandings that students should remember long after the lesson has been taught. They are written in a broad way and may be applicable to multiple lessons. *Do* objectives explain the tasks students will be able to perform or the skills they will be able to demonstrate as a result of the lesson.

Assessment: Teachers and librarians must determine whether students have successfully met the lesson's objectives; if they have not, the lesson may need to be retaught and presented to students in a different way. In the assessment section of each lesson plan, we describe one or more formative assessments that educators may use to determine students' progress toward meeting the lesson objectives. Formative assessments are intended to monitor progress and inform instructional decisions; they are not meant to be collected for a grade as with summative assessments.

Materials: This refers to the texts and resources that educators will need to implement the lesson.

Academic language function: The academic language function is a verb conveying the task that students will perform in the lesson. The verb should be linked to at least one level of Bloom's taxonomy (Anderson et al., 2001). For example, *evaluate* would be an appropriate academic language function if students are making a judgment based on a set of criteria, and *analyze* would be a good choice if students are comparing and contrasting. The academic language function always matches the verb that is used in the lesson plan's central focus.

Language demands: These are the ways that students are using language arts skills during the lesson. They include reading, writing, listening, speaking, viewing, and visually representing. Considering a lesson's language demands may be particularly useful for educators working with English language learners, who may require special support to be successful with a lesson.

Lesson introduction: The purpose of the lesson introduction is to pique students' interest in the lesson content. It is usually a brief activity meant to activate students' prior knowledge and prepare them for the new information they will learn in the lesson. The lesson introduction should also communicate the lesson's purpose or goals in student-friendly terms. Beginning with the lesson introduction, all subsequent sections of the lesson plan template used in this book (except *Differentiation*) are presented as a numbered series of steps.

Instructional input: This means how the teacher will present the new content or skill that students will learn in the lesson. The teacher could deliver a presentation, model how to apply a skill, or share his, her or their thinking about how to complete a process. The purpose of instructional input is to scaffold, or support, students' emerging understanding of the lesson topic.

Work session: In a work session, students have an opportunity to practice applying the knowledge or skill presented in the lesson's instructional input. Students may work independently, in pairs, or in small groups. While the teacher is the center of attention during the instructional input phase of the lesson, the teacher acts as a coach or facilitator during the work session.

Lesson closure: These are steps the teacher will take to wrap up the lesson. A lesson closure may require students to reflect on their learning, and it can also be an opportunity for the teacher to formatively assess their understanding.

Differentiation: When an educator differentiates, he or she makes adjustments to the lesson based on students' interests, readiness, or learning profiles (Tomlinson & Moon, 2013). Teachers can differentiate the following elements of their lessons by interest, readiness, or learning profile: *content*, or what students learn; *process*, or how students make sense of the content; and *product*, or how students demonstrate their learning from the lesson. Each lesson plan presented in this book explains one or more differentiation possibilities.

LOOKING AHEAD

In Chapter 1, we explain what critical literacy is, its theoretical underpinnings, and why it is important. This chapter serves as an important foundation for readers who are not familiar with critical literacy. Starting with Chapter 2, readers will find alternating genre/strategy chapters. We begin the book by sharing information about nonfiction (Chapters 2 and 4). The middle chapters address the different genres of fiction (Chapters 6–10). The final chapters discuss the forms of picture books and graphic novels (Chapters 12 and 14).

1

What Is Critical Literacy?

Scenario 1: *Tasha and her parents are driving home one afternoon when they approach a construction site on the side of the road. A bright orange, diamond-shaped sign is posted to alert drivers. Tasha notices the sign that says, "Men Working." She begins to wonder about the sign's message. "Can't girls be construction workers?" she asks herself. "I can be a construction worker if I want to. So why does the sign say 'men' instead of 'people'? Who wrote this sign? Why don't they think girls can do construction?" These questions nag at Tasha for the whole ride home. Later, she decides to write a letter to her county's transportation department to share her concerns. Tasha suggests the county could create new signs that say "Workers Present," noting this language is more inclusive than "Men Working."*

Scenario 2: *Sam and his family are watching a local broadcast of the evening news when a story airs about a fight between two students at Sam's school. The fight was captured on video by an observer's cell phone, and one of the students sustained severe injuries and was hospitalized. The reporter grimly shares that the fight is the latest in a string of violent acts occurring at Sam's school in the past year. Although Sam is saddened to hear about the fight, he wonders why the news reports only on the bad things happening at school. Just last week, Sam and other members of the Friendship Club raised money to purchase a "buddy bench" for the elementary school playground so lonely children can have a place to seek companionship at recess. "Why can't the news report on a story like this?" Sam wonders. "Why do they always have to say bad things about what happens at my school? People probably think my school is a bad place for kids, but a lot of good stuff happens, too." That night, Sam logs on Twitter and tweets about the Friendship Club's fund-raiser to the news station. "How about you share more stories like this about my school?" he asks.*

Scenario 3: *Carlos is an avid reader. He reads all kinds of books: fantasies about animals, stories about kids facing problems, and biographies about famous people he admires. He has already read most of the books in his classroom library, and he is a frequent visitor to his school's library. As he reads more and more books, Carlos begins to notice that very few of the titles in his classroom's or school's collection include characters or people who identify as Latinx like him. "There are a lot of Latinx kids at this school," Carlos thinks. "So why aren't there more books about people like us? Surely someone is writing books about Latinx people—right?" Carlos begins to research authors who write books featuring Latinx perspectives, and he thinks more about why it is important to have books like this at school. Carlos creates a digital presentation of his research that he plans to share with his teacher and the librarian; he hopes to persuade them to purchase more books about Latinx people for the classroom and the school.*

What do Tasha, Sam, and Carlos have in common? They are all engaging in critical literacy. Although many definitions of "critical literacy" exist, for the purpose of this book, "critical literacy" is considered to be a stance or philosophical belief. Those who are critically literate ask questions about the world around them, take notice when they see instances of inequality and oppression, and engage in actions to promote fairness and justice. Tasha observed that signage at construction sites is biased against females, and she applied her literacy skills to advocate for more inclusive language. Sam was bothered by the negative press at his school and used social media to urge his local news station to focus on positive stories. Carlos noticed the lack of books featuring Latinx people at the library and developed a research-based presentation to advocate for his position. Each of these young people observed an injustice in his or her world and took actions to remedy it.

Critical literacy is about both "reading the world," as Tasha, Sam, and Carlos did when they noticed unjust situations in their schools and communities, and "reading the word," which means considering how texts position people or groups of people in certain ways (Freire & Macedo, 1987, p. 35). Tasha "read the word" when she considered the gender-biased language on a construction sign, and she "read the world" when she realized this language was oppressive to females and something had to be done to rectify it. In critical literacy, a text can be anything that conveys meaning through language or visual signs (McDaniel, 2004). Books, magazines, newspapers, television and radio broadcasts, music, podcasts, advertisements, websites, social media, images, graphics, slogans, and logos can all be considered "texts." From a critical literacy standpoint, texts are never neutral and always convey an ideological perspective (Behrman, 2006; Hall & Piazza, 2008; Leland & Harste, 2004; Luke & Woods, 2009). Texts both support and reproduce a social order that privileges some groups of people and disadvantages others (Janks, 2014).

However, those who are critically literate know how to question the explicit and implicit messages in texts. They take "an active involvement in texts" and resist the idea that texts are neutral (Hall & Piazza, 2008, p. 33). Critically literate readers do the following:

- They "talk back" to texts (Christensen, 2017; Leland, Ociepka, Kuonen, & Bangert, 2018), actively considering the meaning of the text and refusing to passively accept the ideas and ideologies the text conveys.
- They think beyond a surface-level understanding of a text and consider its purpose (McLaughlin & DeVoogd, 2004).

- They view the text from multiple perspectives (Lewison, Flint, & Van Sluys, 2002; McLaughlin & DeVoogd, 2004), analyzing the author's viewpoint and asking whose voices are privileged and whose are marginalized (Creighton, 1997).
- They are attentive to the social and political issues addressed in texts (Lewison et al., 2002).
- They extend their engagement with texts, taking social action to remedy injustice (Lewison et al., 2002; Powell, Cantrell, & Adams, 2001).

Critical literacy is not the same as critical thinking (Lee, 2011), yet critical literacy does demand critical thinking skills. When Tasha thought about the gender bias in the "Men Working" sign, she was *analyzing* its meaning. When Sam saw the news story about the fight and determined the media portrays his school in a negative way, he was *evaluating*, or making a judgment, about how the media depicted his school. When Carlos constructed a digital presentation about the need for more Latinx books in classroom and school libraries, he was *creating* something new. These cognitive processes—analyzing, evaluating, and creating—are higher levels of thinking according to Bloom's revised taxonomy (Anderson et al., 2001). While critical thinking is a component of critical literacy (McDaniel, 2004), critical literacy is distinguished from critical thinking because its aims include working toward equity and social justice, which are not necessarily goals of critical thinking. Indeed, critical literacy extends critical thinking because it involves taking social action (Leland, Harste, Ociepka, Lewison, & Vasquez, 1999). The following sections of this chapter clarify the origins and goals of critical literacy.

THEORETICAL UNDERPINNINGS OF CRITICAL LITERACY

Critical literacy may be understood as a philosophy (McDaniel, 2004). Critical literacy draws from a broad range of perspectives, including reader response theory, media studies, feminism, and critical race theory (Luke & Woods, 2009). However, the work of Paulo Freire is most often connected to critical literacy (Beck, 2005; McDaniel, 2004). Freire (1970/2012) was an educator who worked with people in poverty in his native Brazil. Through engaging in literacy practices, his students gained awareness of the oppressive social and political conditions around them. Freire described several stages of critical literacy: (1) the oppressed become aware of their oppression; (2) the oppressed reconstruct, or transform, how they view themselves and their oppressors; and (3) the oppressed take social action, working to free themselves from the grip of their oppressors. The "oppressed" are those who have been historically silenced or marginalized, including people of color, people in poverty, women, or even children, while "oppressors" can be economic, social, or political institutions or members of dominant groups who wield power in a society. Though Freire's original work was with an oppressed group of people, embracing a critical literacy perspective is for anyone who wants to make the world a more equal and just place for all.

TEACHING CRITICAL LITERACY

In recent decades, Freire's (1970/2012) ideas and pedagogy have been applied in K-12 school settings. However, critical literacy is not a set of instructional strategies (Lee, 2011; McDaniel, 2004) nor a single approach to teaching (Behrman, 2006). Although this book includes lesson plans meant to support young people in their development as critically literate thinkers, the lesson plans are not a prescription for how to "do" critical literacy. Rather, they are intended to illuminate possibilities for engaging children and adolescents in critical literacy. Indeed, methods for teaching critical literacy must be adapted to the classroom or community because what works in one context may not work in another (McLaughlin & DeVoogd, 2004). The social issues that students explore through critical literacy must be relevant to their interests and lived experiences. However, methods and strategies (like the ones in this book) are a starting point to help students become critically literate. Regardless of how critical literacy is taught, all approaches must "share a commitment to the use of literacy for purposes of equity and social justice" (Luke & Woods, 2009, p. 16). In addition, educators should consider that critical literacy is not just for the most advanced students; both very young children and striving learners can also develop a critical literacy stance (Lee, 2011).

According to Beck (2005), critical literacy lessons should be "student-centered and involve lively, sometimes heated, discussion about controversial, provocative issues" (p. 393). Discussion should be prioritized when students are learning how to think from a critical literacy perspective. Freire (1970/2012) himself believed students should be encouraged to think critically about social problems and engage one another in dialogue. Book clubs and literature circles, which are student-centered instructional practices involving conversations about texts, are possible sites for critical literacy in both classrooms and libraries (Forest & Kimmel, 2016; Jocius & Shealy, 2017). For those new to critical literacy, critical conversations with students can be initiated by posing and discussing open-ended questions about texts (Hall & Piazza, 2008). The sidebars appearing in the even-numbered chapters of this book include question stems that teachers, librarians, or students themselves may use to facilitate such discussions.

Children's literature is often used as an entry point for engaging young people in the work of critical literacy (Labadie, Wetzel, & Rogers, 2012). Books can help children and adolescents understand that texts have underlying ideologies (McDaniel, 2004) and demonstrate the unequal power relations existing in the real world (Hall & Piazza, 2008). Books are also useful for introducing conversations about social issues and problems. Certain types of books are particularly helpful when supporting students in their development of a critical literacy stance. Leland et al. (1999) identified characteristics of books that are conducive to teaching critical literacy:

- They portray difference and diversity.
- They depict the lives of people who have been marginalized.
- They demonstrate people engaging in social action.
- They examine how dominant groups and institutions position other people.
- They are complex and do not have simplistic endings.

In addition, Rogers (2002) recommended that texts used to promote critical literacy should relate to students' lives, a particularly salient point when teaching adolescents. The children's and young adult titles described in the pages of this book all adhere to one or more of these criteria.

Those studying librarianship may be familiar with the work of Eliza Dresang (1999), a former youth services librarian and highly regarded scholar who posited Radical Change theory. Dresang described three types of changes that she observed in contemporary books for youth: (1) changing forms and formats, (2) changing perspectives, and (3) changing boundaries. "Type 2" books may include titles featuring multiple perspectives, voices of people who are usually marginalized, and voices of children and teens, who are often silenced. Such books are also compatible with teaching critical literacy in today's classrooms and libraries.

Although numerous resources about critical literacy are available to teachers and librarians, teaching critical literacy is not easy work (Hall & Piazza, 2008; Leland et al., 2018). Beck (2005) identified challenges educators may face when teaching critical literacy. For example, critical literacy can feel overwhelming to educators because there is no single, prescribed method for teaching it, and educators are often tied to scripted curricula, leaving little room for critical literacy. Oslick, Robertson, and Parks (2018) also noted that some educators are reluctant to teach critical literacy because they fear how parents and administrators might react or they feel they are lacking in the authority to teach about social justice issues. While teaching critical literacy is challenging, educators can be assured that critical literacy may be taught in any subject that involves using language or texts (Behrman, 2006). Critical literacy projects can involve students in various other literacies, including reading, writing, speaking, and listening (Powell et al., 2001), thereby matching the demands of many elementary and middle-grade English language arts curricula. Further, the strategies and standards-aligned lesson ideas in this book can help teachers and librarians envision possibilities for incorporating critical literacy in their classrooms or programs in meaningful ways. As described in the concluding section of this chapter, critical literacy is far too important to overlook in today's schools.

IMPORTANCE AND GOALS OF CRITICAL LITERACY

Arguably, teaching students to become critically literate thinkers is more important now than it has ever been. As Leland et al. (2018) contended, "With the explosion of data shared electronically via the internet and social media, the need to question and challenge texts will only continue to grow" (p. 644). Moreover, life in the contemporary United States is rife with social problems. The gap between the wealthy and the poor is wider now than it has been since the years prior to the Great Depression. Fear and xenophobia have captured the hearts and minds of many Americans, leading to political actions that would exclude prospective immigrants from seeking a new start in this country. Unprecedented numbers of women have come forward to share their painful experiences with sexual harassment and assault. People of color continue to face prejudice, discrimination, and institutional racism several decades after the Civil Rights Movement of the 1960s. Janks (2014) observed, "Different times and different places have their own inequities and inequities that merit critical interrogation and intervention" (p. 349). Teaching critical literacy to the current generation of children and adolescents is important not only for the present but also for the future of the nation and the world.

Critical literacy needs to go beyond teaching students to critique texts; it must also invite students to engage in social action (Powell et al., 2001). Participating in social action to remedy social justice issues helps students see that literacy can be used to create change in the world (Behrman, 2006). Gibson (2018) developed a framework called "The Four Legs of the Stool of Social Change" to help educators and students envision possibilities for social action (p. 31). The four "legs" include the following:

- *Philanthropy*, or donating money and goods (e.g., students collecting cans for a food drive)
- *Direct service*, or working with people to provide something they need (e.g., students helping new immigrants practice their English conversational skills)
- *Politics and advocacy*, or working to change policies or raise public awareness of issues (e.g., students organizing a protest to raise awareness about testing practices that are biased against children with disabilities)
- *Community organizing and development*, or helping communities target the causes of social problems and generate solutions (e.g., students assisting an effort to relocate a medical waste facility that is emitting toxins and causing asthma in local children)

While all of these legs are important and necessary, *politics and advocacy* and *community organizing and development* are the most significant in terms of creating sustained social change.

Engaging students in social action may sound like a tall order, but some educators have been successful in their efforts to both teach critical literacy and involve their students in endeavors to enact social change. For example, Young (2009) described a project in which her high school class selected an issue relevant to their lives. Students selected homophobia as many had friends and relatives identifying as gay, lesbian, or bisexual. They researched the issue and thought about the ways homophobia manifested in their own school and community. Their efforts resulted in a school-wide event to raise awareness of homophobia and demonstrate solidarity and respect. Powell et al. (2001) have also provided an excellent model of engaging children in social action. After reading about Black Mountain, Kentucky's highest peak, in a social studies textbook and learning it would soon be strip-mined, fourth graders researched the impact that strip mining would have on both people and the environment. Deciding that strip mining would do more harm than good, students advocated against the mining of Black Mountain. They wrote and spoke to government officials and raised public awareness of the dangers of strip mining. The students' work ultimately led to a compromise that saved thousands of acres of Black Mountain from destruction. These educators clearly supported their students in one of the most important goals of critical literacy: their development as "responsible citizens, able to confront social inequities in their many forms and take action against injustices" (Beck, 2005, p. 399).

As noted previously, critical literacy must be linked to the contexts, interests, and experiences of students in the classroom and community. For this reason, *Genre-Based Strategies to Promote Critical Literacy in Grades 4–8* does not specify social actions that educators and their students should take after reading the children's and young adult titles or implementing the lesson ideas described here. Social actions like public awareness campaigns, protests, book or food drives, and community organizing should be driven by the desires and willingness of students. However, the issues and ideas raised in this book can serve as starting points for initiating students' inquiries and inspiring them to create a more just and equitable world.

2

Informational Books

What in the world is happening in Lucie's class? Books, copies of articles, tablets, and handwritten notes are strewn haphazardly across students' desks. Students are leaning back in their seats and talking—no, arguing—loudly and passionately in small groups scattered around the classroom. Shouldn't Lucie be at the front of the room trying to gain control of her class? Why is she sitting with the students and encouraging them to argue?

Actually, Lucie's lesson is going exactly as planned. Her eighth-grade class is exploring both sides of a controversial issue: "Should the government cull wolves to reduce their population?" Students have been researching this topic using multimodal text sets, and they are applying the information they located to argue both sides of the issue. They are fully engaged in the work of critical literacy as they examine a sociopolitical issue and examine it from multiple perspectives (Lewison, Flint, & Van Sluys, 2002). Lucie's inclusion of informational books in her lesson has helped support students in sustaining a productive, meaningful, and well-informed discussion. In Chapter 3, we will take a closer look at how Lucie developed and facilitated this lesson.

DEFINING NONFICTION

Nonfiction for children is enjoying a heyday. Educators like Lucie have become more aware of the importance of reading nonfiction in school as a result of the Common Core State Standards for English Language Arts and Literacy (National Governors Association Center for Best Practices & Council of Chief State School Officers, 2010), which have placed an increased emphasis on nonfiction. New awards honoring nonfiction, including the Robert F. Sibert Informational Book Medal (first awarded in 2001) and the Young Adult Library Services Association Nonfiction Award (first awarded in 2010), have contributed to the genre's rising prominence. Moreover, the nonfiction books available to today's readers are more appealing to young people than ever before. As literacy educator Donalyn Miller (2013) observed, "The quality and diversity of children's nonfiction [books] have improved drastically over the years" (p. 24). We agree with Miller that nonfiction is a diverse genre; nonfiction spans a variety of topics, forms, and formats. Given this diversity, we find it helpful to categorize nonfiction into two broad subgenres: informational books, the subject of the present chapter, and narrative nonfiction, the subject of Chapter 4.

Nonfiction consists of books that are grounded in facts, the lives of real people, and actual events. When we read a nonfiction book, we read to learn about something that is true in our world as it is today or as it was in the past. For example, we might read nonfiction to learn more about the habitats of sharks or the life of a well-known civil rights activist. As the term "nonfiction" suggests, nonfiction books are *not* fiction: they contain verifiable information, not the stuff of an author's imagination. However, it is important to remember that nonfiction books present "*one* vision of the truth" (Beers & Probst, 2016, p. 19), and a tenet of critical literacy is the possibility of multiple truths (Luke & Woods, 2009).

DEFINING INFORMATIONAL BOOKS

Informational books, which are also called expository books, are written to explain, describe, or inform readers about a real-life topic or phenomenon. In an informational book, the main purpose is to present facts. Narrative nonfiction is also factual, but it has story-like features such as characters, rich descriptions, and a story arc with a beginning, middle, and end (see Chapter 4). Much of contemporary nonfiction for young people falls on a continuum with a mix of explanation and narrative. As an example, *Sea Otter Heroes: The Predators That Saved an Ecosystem* relates facts about a marine ecosystem while simultaneously relating the story of a scientist attempting to solve an ecological mystery. For the purpose of this book, titles that are primarily informational are addressed in this chapter, while titles that adhere more closely to a narrative structure are included in Chapter 4. We have chosen to separate informational books and narrative nonfiction for this text because each subgenre provides distinct opportunities and challenges for critical literacy. Straight informational text is often written in a factual tone that implies a neutral author and includes a presentation of what are considered the established scientific or historical facts about a topic, which invites readers to ponder questions like "what is truth?" or "who gets to decide what the truth is?" Meanwhile, the story-like structure of narrative nonfiction is useful for unpacking why authors choose to emphasize some topics or events while minimizing others ("what, or whose story does the author choose to tell and why?").

Informational books include several types of text features. A table of contents at the beginning of the book informs readers of the topics the books will address. Headings and subheadings within the body of the text organize information and help children anticipate what they will read next. Vocabulary words, particularly technical or scientific terms, are sometimes highlighted, underlined, or italicized, and a glossary defining these words may appear in the back of the book. Also in the back matter, readers can expect to find an index specifying the page number where a topic can be located and a bibliography citing the author's sources. Sidebars may be embedded throughout the main text to provide readers with additional information about a related topic or event. Many informational books published today include "layered text" (Stewart & Young, 2018, p. 17), meaning that the primary text, which contains the main idea, is accompanied by ancillary text, which offers details to support the main idea. This ancillary text may appear in colorful boxes or bubbles to distinguish it from the primary text. However, not all informational books include all of these text features we have described.

In addition, informational books incorporate visuals to support readers in their understanding of topics. *Trash Revolution: Breaking the Waste Cycle* includes many examples. Diagrams and flowcharts are utilized to illustrate processes such as the conversion of wastewater into drinking water, a pie chart displays how many gallons of water are needed to make a pizza in different countries, a timeline displays information about the history of toilets and toilet paper, and a chart compares how much energy is used to make aluminum foil versus plastic wrap. Today's informational books are also celebrated for their vibrant images, which may come in the form of illustrations (e.g., *Trash Revolution*; *We Are Grateful: Otsaliheliga*; *Pipsqueaks, Slowpokes, and Stinkers*) or contemporary or historical photographs (e.g., *Hopping Ahead of Climate Change*; *The Quilts of Gee's Bend*; *The Great Penguin Rescue*). Regardless of the type, children appreciate images that support them in their understanding of the content presented (Hartsfield, 2017).

Often, but not always, informational books do not require reading through the text in a linear fashion from beginning to end. Instead, readers may use features such as the table of contents or the index to move to the page or pages of interest. Readers interested in a particular decade of the lesbian, gay, bisexual, and transgender rights movement can easily turn to the table of contents in *Gay & Lesbian History for Kids: The Century-Long Struggle for LGBT Rights* to locate the information they want. Many informational books also encourage browsing or opening the book to a random page where an image or heading might grab the interest of the reader. For example, *Killer Style: How Fashion Has Injured, Maimed, & Murdered through History* is organized according to three main parts: Horrified Heads, Miserable Middles, and Unlucky Legs. Each part includes short chapters about a particular topic, such as Radium Girls, Strangling Scarves, and Flaming Flannelette. Large headings separate each chapter, allowing readers to flip through the pages to locate an interesting topic. Readers can certainly enjoy the book by reading from beginning to end, but they can also read selectively depending on their interests or purposes for reading.

Informational books are typically organized according to several types of text structures. A "text structure" is a way that authors present or organize information to facilitate readers' understanding of the main idea. The following text structures are present in many of today's nonfiction books for children and young adults:

- *Descriptive*: an event or phenomenon is explained or described.
- *Sequential or chronological*: a series of events are presented in order from beginning to end.
- *Problem/solution*: a problem is posed and a solution is explained.
- *Cause/effect*: an event or situation is presented, and the effect of the event or situation is described.

- *Question/answer*: a series of questions are posed and answered.
- *Compare/contrast*: the differences and similarities between two or more topics are analyzed.

As one might imagine, books written in the sequential or chronological text structure usually must be read from beginning to end in order to make sense to the reader. For example, in *Boys Dancing: From School Gym to Theater Stage*, author George Ancona describes a children's dance program and the steps involved with preparing for a large-scale production. The information presented in this title would feel decontextualized and potentially confusing to the reader if the book was not read from start to finish. However, in a title utilizing the question/answer text structure such as *Not So Different: What You Really Want to Ask about Having a Disability*, readers can dive into the book at any point.

While language arts classrooms often emphasize fiction, many young people prefer nonfiction and its subgenres of informational books and narrative nonfiction. These readers are interested in data or facts about the world around them. They may prefer the kinds of browsing promoted by many informational books and the ability to dip into the middle of a book or to choose their own path through the book based on their interests or previous knowledge about the topic. Young readers like being able to find answers about questions that interest or concern them. They are empowered by the knowledge acquired in such texts as they engage with other texts or in debates surrounding contemporary issues.

EVALUATING INFORMATIONAL BOOKS

Although dozens of outstanding nonfiction titles are published each year, the quality of children's nonfiction can vary. Educators have many resources for locating quality nonfiction at their disposal. Book awards like the Sibert Medal can direct educators toward titles that have been vetted for quality and accuracy; Sidebar 2.1 includes other awards that honor excellence in nonfiction. However, many worthy books that may not receive major awards are published each year. To ensure that excellent books (award-winning or not) make their way into the hands of readers, librarians and teachers responsible for selecting children's books should be familiar with criteria for evaluating nonfiction.

Sidebar 2.1   Nonfiction Book Awards

- Boston Globe-Horn Book Nonfiction Award
- National Council of Social Studies Notable Social Studies Trade Books
- National Council of Teachers of English Orbis Pictus Award
- National Science Teachers Association Outstanding Trade Books
- Robert F. Sibert Informational Book Medal
- Young Adult Library Service Association Nonfiction Award

The credibility of the information presented is a hallmark of a distinguished nonfiction book whether it is narrative or informational. There are two questions to consider when determining a book's credibility. First, we should ask: "Is the author an expert on the subject?" In *We Are Grateful*, author Traci Sorell describes a year in the life of a contemporary Cherokee family. As a member of this group, Sorell is knowledgeable and speaks from an insider perspective; thus, the information she presents is trustworthy. Likewise, in *Not So Different*, author Shane Burcaw explains his personal experiences growing up with spinal muscular atrophy, which makes him an expert on the topic.

However, not all children's book authors will be experts on the subject matter. In these cases, our second question to consider is, "What kind of research did the author do to inform the book?" Diligent and trustworthy nonfiction authors do copious research on their topics by consulting numerous sources and documenting these efforts. For example, in *Sea Otter Heroes*, writer Patricia Newman interviewed the scientists whose work is described in her book, and she also read scientific journal articles they authored to present an informed and factual account to her readers. In addition to these primary sources, she consulted books, other journal articles, and websites on the topics of sea otters and trophic cascade. The robust bibliography in *Sea Otter Heroes* suggests that Newman is a trustworthy source of information although she is not a scientist or biology expert herself.

When evaluating nonfiction (especially when the author is not an expert), we should be wary (1) when a book does not have a bibliography or (2) when a book has a slim bibliography or a bibliography relying on questionable sources. These situations suggest the author did not complete any research, did not complete research with reliable sources, or did not care enough to document the research. All of these circumstances are discourteous to the nonfiction reader, who deserves to understand the credibility of the information presented.

Accuracy is critical when evaluating nonfiction. A nonfiction book that presents inaccurate information defeats one of the main reasons why we read nonfiction: to learn facts about our world. Once again, a nonfiction book's bibliography can help us evaluate whether the information in the book is accurate. Authors who use multiple sources in their research are able to corroborate facts through consulting various sources. Moreover, much like in the childhood game of "telephone," authors consulting primary sources such as firsthand accounts (e.g., interviews, letters, diaries), newspaper articles, and scientific journal articles are more likely to "get the facts straight" than authors relying on secondary or tertiary sources like textbooks or encyclopedias. In addition, diligent authors will often ask a subject matter expert to vet their manuscript before it is published to ensure its accuracy. Usually, authors will acknowledge the assistance of these experts in an author's note or acknowledgment section in the book's back matter.

Text features such as diagrams, tables, charts, maps, and timelines should be included in the evaluation of informational texts. When applicable, readers look for these features and should evaluate their organization, clarity, and source. Text features that seem overly stylistic rather than straightforward may be confusing to children (Hartsfield, 2017). Images, whether they are photographs or illustrations, should be sized and of sufficient quality to discern their details. The purpose of an image in a nonfiction book is to communicate information, and when an image is difficult to interpret, it has limited utility for readers. An image's location near the relevant text and the inclusion of captions and source notes as applicable are also important to consider.

Given that one characteristic of an informational book is the ability to locate specific information in a text, the organization of the text is important to evaluate. Is the content arranged in a manner where it is accessible to the reader? Decisions about how to divide up the content and how to name sections and chapters are important, but within chapters, the use of headings and subheadings may aid readers in the location of particular information. The presence of a table of contents acquainting readers with how the content is organized enables them to find information and make decisions about how to sequence reading. Furthermore, a detailed and intuitive index is essential in a quality informational book.

The writing in an informational book should be accessible for the intended reader. Vocabulary should represent the disciplinary vocabulary rather than generic or novice terminology, and authors demonstrate courtesy to readers when they define this vocabulary either within the text or in a glossary appearing in the book's back matter. Voice is also important. Informational books can be informative *and* entertaining. *Trash Revolution* is an excellent example of an informational book with an engaging and humorous voice. For example, in a sidebar entitled "Figuring Out Your Foodprint," author Erica Fyvie jokes with readers and addresses them directly: "Do you carrot all about your lunch waste? (Is that cheesy?)" What could easily be a boring, dull book about the fate of trash is enlivened by the author's use of puns and conversational language. With such care given to presenting information in engaging ways, it is no surprise that the nonfiction genre is enjoying a well-deserved increase in popularity.

READING INFORMATIONAL BOOKS WITH A CRITICAL LITERACY LENS

Many informational books are outstanding for the purpose of engaging students in critical literacy. Some books present social issues that can initiate conversations with students and invite them to consider the multiple sides of an issue. In *Killer Style*, readers learn about how clothing designs and styles have often harmed the most vulnerable members of society. For example, many people have likely worn a pair of sand-blasted jeans because of the popularity of distressed denim styles. However, the workers who sandblast jeans sometimes work in poorly ventilated environments and are given inadequate facial protection. Consequently, they inhale silica particles, and some develop silicosis, a lung disease that can be fatal. Topics like this can facilitate critical conversations with students. Educators might ask: "Who benefits from sandblasting denim? Who loses? Why don't companies provide workers with safer environments if they must sandblast jeans? Is one person's desire to buy sandblasted jeans more important than another person's right to a safe work environment? Why do you think you haven't heard about this issue before? Who gains from the silence surrounding this issue?"

> **Sidebar 2.2 Question Stems for Informational Books**
>
> - Why do you think the author was motivated to write about this topic? What does the author want you to think or do as a result of reading this book?
> - Who is most qualified to write about the content of this book? Is the author a trustworthy and credible source?
> - How do the facts presented in the book connect to what you already know? Do these facts contradict or confirm your prior knowledge?
> - What new information did you learn as a result of reading this book? Why do you think you did not encounter this information before?

Other books promote critical literacy by illuminating the different sides of an issue. For example, in *Camp Panda: Helping Cubs Return to the Wild* by Catherine Thimmesh, readers learn about how scientists and conservationists are taking new approaches to reintroduce captive-born pandas into the wild. However, Thimmesh also presents the views of those opposing these conservation efforts. Dissenters argue that nature should be allowed to take its course without human intervention, and the money spent on saving giant pandas could be used for other purposes. By sharing both sides of the argument, Thimmesh shows readers the complexity of social, political, and environmental issues. Likewise, in *Up for Sale: Human Trafficking and Modern Slavery*, author Alison Marie Behnke shares the perspectives of both trafficking victims and traffickers. While readers will likely have empathy for the trafficking victims, Behnke's inclusion of the traffickers' perspectives helps readers understand the sociopolitical issues driving the traffickers' actions.

Still other books encourage critical literacy by introducing underrepresented topics. In *Pipsqueaks, Slowpokes, and Stinkers: Celebrating Animal Underdogs*, author Melissa Stewart describes animals that might seem slow, lazy, or smelly, but they all have characteristics enabling their survival. For instance, after noting that a walrus can have more than 400 pounds of fat, Stewart asks readers to stop and ponder: "Think these plump lumps should go on a diet?" But when they turn the page, readers learn this thick layer of fat assists the walrus with staying warm in the cold ocean water. In addition, in *Boys Dancing*, readers follow a group of four boys as they learn to dance and participate in a performance. It is easy to enter a library and locate a book about females who have achieved successful careers in dancing, but it is much more difficult to find a book about males involved in dance. Books like these invite readers to question their assumptions and consider why topics such as "boring" animals or male dancers receive less attention than topics such as cute, fast, and ferocious animals or female dancers.

As noted in Chapter 1, social activism is a significant goal of critical literacy work. Some informational books suggest realistic ways for young people to become involved in creating positive change. In *Zoo Scientists to the Rescue*, which is about three zoo scientists working to study and save endangered species, Patricia Newman identifies several possibilities for children and adolescents to become involved in conservation efforts. For example, Newman describes smartphone apps that can help consumers identify sustainably harvested products and explains simple steps people can take to conserve water and energy. *Eat This!: How Fast Food Marketing Gets You to Buy Junk (And How to Fight Back)* by Andrea Curtis is another title inviting readers to take action. Curtis informs readers they can take a stand against the proliferation of junk food by creating a class cookbook of healthy recipes, planting a school garden to create access to fresh produce, and writing letters to convince administrators to make schools ad-free zones.

Because nonfiction books present facts, readers might think they are neutral or free of bias. Although some authors of informational books do present multiple sides of an issue, such as Catherine Thimmesh in *Camp Panda*, those who have adopted a critical literacy stance understand that texts are always colored by the perspectives of their authors. In other words, there is no such thing as a "neutral" book even if its purpose is to present facts. Educators can support students in this understanding by developing multimodal nonfiction text sets to share in classrooms and libraries. A text set is a collection of resources about a topic. These resources may include books, articles in periodicals, websites, images or graphics, videos, podcasts, and songs. A text set is multimodal when it includes resources in various modalities, meaning students can engage with the topic by reading, listening, and/or viewing. Multimodal text sets are a valuable instructional tool because they allow educators to differentiate instruction and engage students in higher-order thinking (Hartsfield & Maxwell, 2018).

Multimodal nonfiction text sets also promote the development of critical literacy skills. When readers examine the resources in text sets, they encounter multiple perspectives on the same topic. In addition, by comparing and contrasting the information appearing in different text set resources, readers are able to see that authors are selective with the information they choose to present and omit. They begin to understand that texts are always slanted toward a particular viewpoint, however subtle or implicit. Further, by examining resources in a text set, readers can become more aware of the techniques authors use to convince readers of their viewpoint. In Chapter 3, we share a text set examining the controversial issue of culling, or systematically and intentionally eliminating, wolf populations in the United States and Canada. One of the resources in the text set is an article called "Saving America's Wolves," which addresses readers as "you" and encourages them to take the perspective of a wolf. Although the article does attempt to explain why some people want to cull wolves, the presentation of information through the second-person point of view is a technique utilized to persuade readers that killing wolves is problematic. Readers can make this connection when they observe that other resources in this text set are presented in a more "objective" third-person point of view.

Ready-made text sets on a variety of topics can easily be found by searching online, but it is important for educators to have the "know-how" to develop their own text sets to suit their instructional goals and students' interests. Hartsfield and Maxwell (2018) identify steps educators can take to develop quality multimodal text sets:

1. Determine which learning standards the text set should address.
2. Develop learning objectives related to the purpose of using the text set.

3. Write guiding questions that can be answered by consulting the resources included in the text set. For example, when designing the text set featured in Chapter 3, our guiding question was, "What are the reasons why wolves should or should not be culled?"

4. Search for text set resources. The school librarian can offer invaluable assistance with this step. Educators may utilize databases such as the Children's Comprehensive Database or NoveList to locate books about the desired topic. A multimodal text set should encompass different kinds of sources, so educators are also encouraged to look for magazine articles, websites, films, and podcasts.

5. Narrow down the text set resources. Consider whether the potential resources can help students answer the guiding question from Step 3, and evaluate whether the resources align with the standards and learning objectives. Make sure the resources selected for the text set are accessible to students at a range of levels. They should also be balanced to the extent possible, meaning they should not overrepresent or underrepresent a particular point of view. Although there is no "magic number" of how many resources should be included in a text set, we recommend a minimum of five resources.

By following these steps, educators are equipped to develop multimodal text sets addressing a range of topics and issues. In the next chapter, we provide an example of a multimodal text set and explain how teachers can utilize text sets to engage students with examining the different sides of a complex issue.

ANNOTATED BIBLIOGRAPHY

Ancona, George. *Boys Dancing: From School Gym to Theater Stage*. 2017. 48 pp. Candlewick. 9780763682026

Vivid photographs accompany this account of four boys preparing for a community dance production, an underrepresented topic in books for youth.

Ancona, George. *Can We Help?: Kids Volunteering to Help Their Communities*. 2015. 48 pp. Candlewick. 9780763673673

Children can make the world a better place in many ways, from knitting scarves and hats for people in need to helping deliver meals for homebound people. This book depicts real children engaged in volunteering.

Behnke, Alison Marie. *Up for Sale: Human Trafficking and Modern Slavery*. 2014. 72 pp. Twenty-First Century Books. 9781467716116

Young readers may be surprised to learn that slavery has persisted into modern times in the form of human trafficking. This short chapter book discusses several types of contemporary slavery across the world, including sex trafficking, labor trafficking, and child labor.

Burcaw, Shane. *Not So Different: What You REALLY Want to Ask about Having a Disability*. Carr, Matt. 2017. 40 pp. 9781626727717

This question-and-answer-format book offers readers a frank discussion about what it is like to live with a disability from the perspective of Shane Burcaw, a social activist born with spinal muscular atrophy. Burcaw's humor and candor make a "taboo" topic accessible to readers of all ages.

Castaldo, Nancy. *Back from the Brink: Saving Animals from Extinction*. 2018. 176 pp. HMH Books for Young Readers. 9780544953437
This book profiles several species, including gray wolves, California condors, and whooping cranes, and the reasons why each species has nearly become extinct. The book can raise questions and critical conversations about the impact of human activity on wild animals.

Collard, Sneed B. *Hopping Ahead of Climate Change: Snowshoe Hares, Science, and Survival*. 2016. 64 pp. Bucking Horse Books. 9780984446087
How is climate change impacting snowshoe hares? The author explores how global warming has contributed to the survival capabilities of animals and addresses what scientists are doing about the problem.

Curtis, Andrea. *Eat This!: How Fast Food Marketing Gets You to Buy Junk (And How to Fight Back)*. Collins, Peggy. 2018. 36 pp. Red Deer Press. 9780889955325
Marketers use many tactics to encourage kids to eat junk food, such as enticing them with free toys, fun mascots, and punchy ads. Peppered with facts and cases from countries around the world, this book teaches kids how marketers influence their thinking and what kids can do to challenge them.

Fyvie, Erica. *Trash Revolution: Breaking the Waste Cycle*. Slavin, Bill. 2018. 64 pp. Kids Can Press. 9781771380782
What happens to the items in a backpack—plastic water bottles, aluminum cans, leftover food, dirty gym clothes—when they are thrown away? This title addresses how commonly used items are made, how much energy is used to make them, how long it takes them to decompose, and what they might become if they are recycled.

Levinson, Cynthia, & Levinson, Sanford. *Fault Lines in the Constitution: The Framers, Their Fights, and the Flaws That Affect Us Today*. 2017. 235 pp. Peachtree Publishers. 9781561459452
The authors take a decided point of view: that many of the constitutional issues we face today, including who can vote, who can run for office, who is represented, and who is not, can be traced to the way the Constitution was originally framed and the debates surrounding the formation of the original document. Historical details are juxtaposed with current events and a debate about how we might change.

Markle, Sandra. *The Great Penguin Rescue: Saving the African Penguins*. 2018. 48 pp. Millbrook Press. 9781512413151
Human activity has caused a major decline in southern Africa's penguin population. Readers learn how scientists, conservationists, and volunteers are working together to save the future of this at-risk species.

Markle, Sandra. *The Great Rhino Rescue: Saving the Southern White Rhinos*. 2019. 48 pp. Millbrook Press. 9781512444360
Southern white rhinos are endangered once again due to human activity, and scientists and others are working to save them. Readers will consider how human wants and needs should be weighed against the rights of animals.

McMahon, Serah-Marie, & David, Alison Matthews. *Killer Style: How Fashion Has Injured, Maimed, & Murdered through History*. Wilson, Gillian. 2019. 48 pp. Owl Kids Press. 9781771472531
Familiar phrases like "fashion victim" and "fashion disaster" take on new meanings in this book about how clothing, accessories, and makeup have maimed people over the centuries. It addresses social justice issues such as the "flaming flannelette" marketed to working-class families as well as disasters in clothing factories that have disfigured or killed workers.

Newman, Patricia. *Sea Otter Heroes: The Predators That Saved an Ecosystem*. 2017. 56 pp. Millbrook Press. 9781512426311

The seagrass in California's Elkhorn Slough remains healthy despite chemical runoff from nearby farms. Readers learn how sea otters are responsible for preserving the health of the ecosystem. This book addresses the impact of humans on the environment and the role of various organisms in preserving the well-being of an ecosystem.

Newman, Patricia. *Zoo Scientists to the Rescue*. Crawley, Annie. 2018. 64 pp. Millbrook Press. 9781512415711

This book profiles three zoo scientists whose research improves the survival of endangered animals living in both captivity and the wild. Profiled species include orangutans, black-footed ferrets, and black rhinos.

Pohlen, Jerome. *Gay & Lesbian History for Kids: The Century-Long Struggle for LGBT Rights*. 2015. 192 pp. Chicago Review Press. 9781613730829

Accompanied by many visuals and a variety of text features, this title relates the history of the lesbian, gay, bisexual, and transgender (LGBT) rights movement. Though most attention is given to twentieth-century events, the presence of LGBT people in world history prior to 1900 is also addressed.

Rubin, Susan Goldman. *The Quilts of Gee's Bend*. 2017. 56 pp. Abrams Books for Young Readers. 9781419721311

Accompanied by historical photos, this book chronicles the artwork produced by the women of Gee's Bend, an African American community located in rural Alabama. It can invite conversations with children about what constitutes art and which groups of people are/are not traditionally perceived as artists and why.

Sorell, Traci. *We Are Grateful: Otsaliheliga*. Lessac, Frané. 2018. 32 pp. Charlesbridge. 9781580897723

Each season brings a new reason to feel grateful for the Cherokee family depicted in this book. This title offers a glimpse into contemporary Cherokee life, an under-represented perspective in books for youth.

Stewart, Melissa. *Pipsqueaks, Slowpokes, and Stinkers: Celebrating Animal Underdogs*. Laberis, Stephanie. 2018. 32 pp. Peachtree Publishers. 9781561459360

Instead of focusing on strong, fierce, and fast animals, this title invites readers to consider the strengths of animals that are often overlooked. Readers learn that seemingly weird or quirky characteristics can actually be critical to an animal's survival.

Thimmesh, Catherine. *Camp Panda: Helping Cubs Return to the Wild*. 2018. 60 pp. Houghton Mifflin Harcourt. 9780544818910

Giant pandas are beloved across the world, but human population growth has pushed them out of their habitat and decimated their population. Scientists and conservationists are taking new approaches to reintroduce captive-born pandas into the wild.

3

Examining Multiple Perspectives with Multimodal Text Sets (Lesson Plan)

In Chapter 2, we described the value of using multimodal text sets to help students explore significant issues in the content areas. Here, we turn to an instructional approach that teachers can use in conjunction with text sets: the Structured Academic Controversy (Estes & Mintz, 2016). In this approach, students work in teams to analyze multiple sides of a controversy using a variety of resources provided by the teacher.

Setting up a Structured Academic Controversy requires thoughtful planning by educators and a substantial amount of class time. For example, the lesson plan we share in this chapter may require an entire week of class sessions. According to Estes and Mintz (2016), planning a Structured Academic Controversy begins with determining a question that addresses a controversial issue. Here, our question is, "Should the government cull wolves to reduce their population?" After selecting the question, educators must collect resources that can help students examine the different sides of the controversy. Estes and Mintz recommend educators organize these resources into "pro" and "con" packets. Yet in the present lesson, students are asked to examine resources in a text set that have not been explicitly identified by the teacher as pro or con. This is because students are asked to make this determination on their own. In this lesson, students must consider "Is this resource pro, con, or neither?" and "What evidence from this text could be used to support or undermine my argument?"

Next, students are divided into small groups. Teams of four are ideal according to Estes and Mintz (2016). Each team is then split in half. Half of the team is assigned to examine the pro side of the controversy, and the other half of the team is assigned to look at the con side of the controversy. Students' actual opinions of the controversial issue should not factor into these assignments; all students will eventually argue both sides of the controversy. The split teams then work on reading or viewing the resources in the text set, collecting evidence in support of their assigned position. It may be helpful for students to take notes on a graphic organizer such as the one shown in Figure 3.1.

After consulting their resources and constructing their arguments, both sides of each team join together. Each side has a turn presenting its argument, and students

Use this graphic organizer to take notes as you examine the resources in the text set. Make sure you indicate the source of the information included in your notes.

Essential question:

Should the government cull wolves to reduce their population?

Your assigned position (circle one): **In favor**   **Opposed**

Who is in favor of this position?	Why are people or groups in favor of this position?	In what ways do animals, the environment, people, or groups benefit from taking this position?

Figure 3.1   Structured Academic Controversy Graphic Organizer

From *Genre-Based Strategies to Promote Critical Literacy in Grades 4–8* by Danielle E. Hartsfield and Sue C. Kimmel. Santa Barbara, CA: Libraries Unlimited. Copyright © 2020.

should cite evidence from the text set in support of their positions. After both sides have made their case, the team engages in open discussion. Each side continues advocating for its assigned position and attempts to undermine the arguments made by the opposing side through questioning and making rebuttals.

Following the conclusion of the open discussion, students switch sides. Now, students who initially argued the pro side must argue the con side and vice versa. They return to the resources in the text set and locate evidence in support of their new position. After preparing their arguments, both sides of the team join together once again. Each side presents its argument using evidence and ideas from the text set. When the presentations have been made, the team then works together to develop a joint position statement—a compromise—synthesizing key points from both sides of the controversy. These statements are shared with the whole class at the lesson conclusion.

As it is used in the lesson described in this chapter, the Structured Academic Controversy approach addresses several characteristics of critical literacy work that we described in Chapter 1. For example, we suspect that many young people might reply "Of course not!" when asked the question "Should the government cull wolves to reduce their population?" After all, shooting wolves from helicopters, poisoning them, and trapping them seem inhumane. By taking a deeper dive into the issue with the Structured Academic Controversy, students are moving beyond their initial assumptions, learning about different sides of the issue, and thereby considering multiple perspectives. Furthermore, students recognize that texts are not neutral. Because they are using the same text set of materials to construct *both* sides of an argument, they begin to understand that people can selectively include or exclude information from the same sources to suit their own purposes. In addition, students' examination of the text set will inevitably help them see the political and financial motivations behind government-sponsored killings of wolves, prompting them to focus on sociopolitical issues. Finally, after teams of students generate their joint position statements, the lesson can be extended by having students take action. Students may possibly decide that the government should stop killing wolves. Instead, more national parks could be created, giving wolves more space to roam and moving them further away from people, livestock, and domestic animals. Students could write letters and petition lawmakers to advocate for their position, an authentic activity that connects critical literacy to the real world.

The lesson plan on the following pages describes how Lucie engages her students in critical literacy by utilizing a multimodal text set with the Structured Academic Controversy instructional approach. Lucie teaches her lesson over a five-day period. On the first day, students participate in a gallery walk about the topic—culling wolves—to activate their prior knowledge. They also begin to examine the resources in the multimodal text set. On the second and third days, students continue studying the resources, and they construct their arguments and share their presentations in their small teams. On the fourth day, the students return to the text set and construct and present an argument for the opposing side. Finally, on the last day of the lesson, the teams work together to develop their position statement and share it with the class. They also plan the action steps they would take to advocate for their stance in the world outside of school. Table 3.1 demonstrates the steps and rationale of Lucie's lesson plan, and the resources included in the text set that her students examine appear in the "Materials" section. While this lesson includes standards for the English language arts, it could easily be applied in a science class in which students study human intervention and animal populations.

Table 3.1   Lesson Plan

Central focus: Students will *analyze* resources in a text set to construct an argument about a controversial issue.	**Subject:** English language arts
Grade: 8	**Classroom Context:** Whole group (with students working in teams of four)

Standards

CCSS.ELA-LITERACY.SL.8.1: Engage effectively in a range of collaborative discussions (one-on-one, in groups, and teacher-led) with diverse partners on grade 8 topics, texts, and issues, building on others' ideas and expressing their own clearly. a. Come to discussions prepared, having read or researched material under study; explicitly draw on that preparation by referring to evidence on the topic, text, or issue to probe and reflect on ideas under discussion.

CCSS.ELA-LITERACY.SL.8.4: Present claims and findings, emphasizing salient points in a focused, coherent manner with relevant evidence, sound valid reasoning, and well-chosen details; use appropriate eye contact, adequate volume, and clear pronunciation.

Objectives

Students will *know* the arguments made by stakeholders supporting and opposing the actions of the American and Canadian governments to cull gray wolves.

Students will *understand* that controversial issues have many stakeholders who are motivated by different interests.

Students will *be able to* synthesize and cite evidence from multiple sources in support of an argument. Students will *be able to* construct and present an oral argument using text-based evidence.

Assessment: As students make their presentations in Step 12, the teacher will assess them through observation using the Participation Checklist (see Figure 3.2 at the end of this lesson plan). Although the teacher's primary concern is assessing students' ability to examine multiple sources and synthesize their findings into a cohesive oral argument, the teacher may also assess for previously learned skills such as making eye contact, speaking clearly, and working cooperatively. In addition, the teacher may collect students' graphic organizers (Figure 3.1) to determine if students have used multiple sources to build their positions.

Materials

- Posters (see Step 1)
- Graphic organizer for each student (see Figure 3.1)
- Checklist to use for each student (see Figure 3.2)
- Text set

The text set consists of the following materials. At least two copies of each print item should be available per student team. The videos may be linked to the class website; students will need tablets or laptops to access these.

Canadian Broadcasting Company. (2015, February 11). *Wolf cull in B.C.: A war on the wolf* [Video file]. Retrieved from https://www.youtube.com/watch?v=d0yjvKuLCek

- This video offers multiple perspectives of the controversy over culling wolves in British Columbia.

Castaldo, N.F. (2018). *Back from the brink*. New York, NY: Houghton Mifflin Harcourt.

- Chapter 3, "Wolves in the Wild," is used for the purpose of this lesson. The chapter explains why wolves, which are apex predators, are necessary for preserving the balance of the ecosystem. It also introduces the controversy about culling wolves and explains why some people want the wolf population reduced.

Klein, A. (2016, October 22). "To kill or not to kill?" *New Scientist, 232*(3096), 18–19.

- This essay examines the ethics of culling animals, including wolves. Its complexity makes it suitable for readers who need a challenge.

Lewis, K. (2018, May). "Saving America's Wolves." *Scholastic SCOPE, 66*(8), 4–10.

- Told in the second person from a wolf's point of view, this article explains why people are afraid of wolves and what happens when a wolf disappears from an ecosystem. It is recommended for striving readers though it has information that all students can use to build their arguments.

The Ecologist. (2013, March 13). *Shades of gray: America's wolf dilemma* [Video file]. Retrieved from https://www.youtube.com/watch?v=AydbYkWP1zk

- This video shares the perspectives of different stakeholders in the controversy over culling wolves in the western United States.

Academic language function: Analyze	**Language demands:** Reading texts, viewing videos, making an oral argument, listening to an argument

Lesson introduction

1. Before the lesson begins, the teacher places posters around the classroom; they can be large post-it pages or easel paper. Each poster has one of the following questions: *Is it right for the government to kill wolves to reduce their population (culling)? Who benefits when wolves are killed? Who loses out when wolves are killed? Who do you think are the stakeholders in the controversy about culling wolves? Why do you think the controversy over culling wolves has become a political issue instead of a conservation issue? Whose voices do you think could be missing from the controversy?*

(*Continued*)

Table 3.1   Lesson Plan (Continued)

2. The teacher introduces the lesson to students. "We have been working on using information and evidence from texts to support our points in discussions. We are going to continue practicing this skill, but this week, we are going to examine an ongoing controversy and use text-based evidence to make an oral argument. In particular, we will study and present arguments about the government-sponsored culling of wolves in the United States and Canada. Does anyone know about this controversy and would be willing to share?" The teacher calls on students to respond. If no students respond or if their responses are inaccurate, the teacher explains, "Culling is when people intentionally kill an animal population to reduce their numbers. Although some species of wolves, like the gray wolf, have nearly gone extinct at some points in time, wolves in the United States and Canada have been culled by the government. Some people think that wolves threaten livestock and consume too many elk, deer, and caribou so there are fewer available to human hunters. We are going to examine both sides of the controversy by studying multiple sources in a text set from different perspectives."

3. The teacher says, "We will start by activating your thinking about this issue. You may notice that around the classroom, there are several posters featuring questions about the wolf culling controversy. For the next twenty minutes, I would like you to circulate around to each poster and write down what you think. It is okay if you do not know the answer. Take your best guess and record your ideas." The students begin moving around the classroom and writing their ideas on the posters. The students do not need to go in a particular order as they respond to the questions on the posters.

4. After the time is up, the teacher reviews what students have written on the posters and synthesizes common ideas. The teacher says, "Now we are going to begin reading the sources in our text set. As you read, think back to what you wrote on the posters to see if your ideas were correct."

Instructional input

5. The teacher introduces the essential question of the Structured Academic Controversy to the class: *Should the government cull wolves to reduce their population?* Then, the teacher organizes the students into teams of four. The teacher says, "Each team of four students is going to be divided into two sides, so you will be working with one other person within your team. One side of the team is going to argue in favor of culling wolves, and the other side of the team is going to argue against culling wolves. I am going to assign each partner group to a side, but do not worry—you will have the chance to argue both sides of the controversy by the time we finish with this lesson at the end of the week." The teacher assigns each partner set within each team to a side of the argument (*for* or *against*). The teacher gives each team the text set materials (multiple copies of the book, multiple copies of the magazine articles, and tablets or laptops for viewing the videos).

6. The teacher hands out the graphic organizers (see Figure 3.1). The teacher says, "I would like you to work with your partner to read Chapter 3 of *Back from the Brink*, the book in the text set we are working with. This chapter will give you information about gray wolves and how they have nearly become extinct in the United States because of hunting and habitat loss. It will also introduce you to the controversy over culling wolves. As you read, please use your graphic organizer to take notes. When you have finished reading the chapter, you and your partner may then begin examining the other materials in the text set. The text set includes a website, two videos, and two magazine articles. Try to read or view as many of these resources as you can today and during our next few days of this lesson, but do not worry if you cannot read or see all of them. You may read or view the resources in any order that you want." (Note: The teacher should post written instructions for this step in case students forget what to do when they finish reading the book chapter.)

Work session

7. Students work with their partners within their team to read and view the resources in the text set and take notes in support of their assigned side on their graphic organizer. This step may require multiple class sessions.

8. After both sides of each team have had ample time to construct their arguments using the text set materials, the teacher instructs each partner set to give an oral presentation of their argument to the opposing side of the team. The teacher may set a time limit (e.g., each side receives ten minutes to make its argument). Both sides (partner sets) of each team make their oral arguments. All students should use their notes and evidence from the text set to support the points made in their arguments.

Students on the *in favor* side may make the following arguments:

- Excessive numbers of wolves leave fewer deer, elk, and caribou for people to hunt, and some people depend on game to feed their families.
- Fewer deer, elk, and caribou hurt hunters and people who make their living as taxidermists.
- Wolves kill livestock belonging to ranchers and farmers, and sometimes, the government has to compensate these people for livestock killed by wolves.
- Animals like deer, elk, and caribou have as much of a right to life as wolves. Wolves are their predators.

Students on the *against* side may make these arguments:

- The wolf population is already controlled by various natural causes such as sickness or injury.
- Wolves are apex predators. They are necessary contributors to a healthy ecosystem.
- Wolves draw tourists and bring in money.
- People make decisions on behalf of wolves in the interest of politics instead of conservation.
- People are afraid of wolves and have vilified them for ages, but most wolves avoid people.

(Continued)

Table 3.1 Lesson Plan (Continued)

9. Following the arguments from each side, the teams of students participate in an open discussion. They ask each other questions and make rebuttals to the opposing side's ideas. The teacher emphasizes that the opposing partner sets within each team are expected to disagree, but they must do so respectfully.

10. After the open discussion, the teacher reassigns the partner sets within each team to the other side of the argument (e.g., if a partner set argued *in favor* of culling wolves, they will now argue *against* culling wolves). Steps 6–8 are repeated. The teacher reminds students that although they are reading and viewing the same sources a second time, they are viewing them from a new perspective.

11. On the final day of the lesson, the teacher says, "You have reviewed the materials in our text set multiple times, and you have argued both sides of the controversy about whether the government should cull the wolf population. Now, your team will work cooperatively to generate a position statement that includes ideas from both sides of the argument. A *position statement* means that you will prepare a short speech about what you think is the best solution to the wolf culling controversy. When you construct your position statement, you must consider all of the stakeholders: the deer, elk, and caribou; the hunters; the taxidermists; the farmers and ranchers; the conservationists; the scientists; and the wolves themselves. What is a compromise that could make each stakeholder happy? Your group should also list the action steps that you will take to advocate for your position in the real world. Will you write a letter to the government? Create a petition? Write an essay to persuade people? Think about what you can do to take action, and you will have time in class next week to implement your ideas." The students begin working cooperatively in their teams to create their position statements and list their action ideas.

Lesson closure

12. After each team has had time to construct its position statements and list of action steps, the teams share their ideas with the whole class and discuss similarities and differences.

Differentiation: Differentiation is built into this lesson plan through the use of a multimodal text set. The print-based materials are written at a variety of reading levels so there are accessible and challenging texts available to all students. The multimodal nature of the text set (books, videos) ensures there are resources to accommodate students' varying preferences for learning information.

Striving learners are supported in this lesson through the use of a graphic organizer to take notes and the opportunity to work with a partner.

Learners who are ready for a challenge may be encouraged to locate additional resources to support their argument or undermine the opposing argument.

Student Name: _____

_____ The student cites evidence or information from the text set when stating points during the presentation.

_____ The student refers to multiple sources from the text set when stating points during the presentation.

_____ The student's argument accurately reflects the perspectives of individuals, groups, and other stakeholders involved in the controversy.

_____ The student works cooperatively and equitably with his, her, or their partner before and during the presentation.

_____ The student speaks audibly and clearly and makes eye contact when sharing during the presentation.

_____ The student asks questions or makes rebuttals to undermine the points made by the opposing side of the team.

_____ The student listens respectfully and attentively to members of the opposing side of the team.

_____ The student works cooperatively and demonstrates a willingness to compromise when constructing a joint position statement with his, her, or their team.

Figure 3.2 Participation Checklist: Structured Academic Controversy

MODIFYING THE LESSON PLAN

Critical literacy practices should be based on the classroom context (McLaughlin & DeVoogd, 2004). What issues do students care about? What matters to them in their school and community? What injustices do they encounter in their everyday lives? While a lesson like this one about wolf culling may particularly resonate with students living in states like Montana, Idaho, and Wyoming—where wolves exist in the wild—students in other locales may be less interested in the topic. Educators should select topics and materials for multimodal text sets that are relevant to students' lives, interests, and passions. For more text set ideas and where to locate ready-made text sets, readers are encouraged to refer to Hartsfield and Maxwell (2018).

Although this lesson is written for eighth-grade students, its structure can be adapted for other grade levels. For example, a teacher could allow the class to discuss and determine a controversy that they would like to explore for the purpose of the lesson. Allowing students to choose ensures they will select a developmentally appropriate topic that will interest and motivate them. Of course, teachers can adjust the content of their text sets according to the topic of the academic controversy, students' reading levels or readiness, and students' preferred learning modalities. While our example text set includes books, videos, and a website, other text sets might include other kinds of sources like podcasts to appeal to different learners. Finally, teachers may adjust the level of scaffolding they provide as students interact with the resources in the text set to construct their arguments. In this lesson, it is assumed that eighth-grade learners have previous experience with using resources to take notes and text-based evidence to support their points. Teachers of younger students may need to model these skills prior to the lesson and provide one-on-one assistance as students engage in their research.

4

Narrative Nonfiction and Biographies

Students in Jacob's sixth grade U.S. history class are studying the antebellum period. As we peek into Jacob's classroom, students are poring over a photocopied page of a biography about President Andrew Jackson. Highlighters and pens are in their hands, and we can see the students nudge each other, whispering and pointing to the text. Jacob's students are marking up the page with notes, comments, and questions as they act as "bias detectives," applying the close reading skills they have been learning to unpack the author's stance toward Jackson. What does the author want the students to think about Jackson? What word choices does the author use to describe Jackson? What events from Jackson's life does the author highlight, and what events does the author leave out? Narrative nonfiction books, including biographies, afford rich opportunities to learn how to read from a critically literate stance. In Chapter 5, we will return to Jacob's classroom to learn more about how teachers can use the strategy of close reading to help students examine narrative nonfiction texts critically.

DEFINING NARRATIVE NONFICTION

"Narrative" is another term for "story." Narrative nonfiction, therefore, is nonfiction that shares characteristics with stories. Also called "literary nonfiction," narrative nonfiction includes contemporary and historical figures (like characters in a story) and a sequence of events with rising action, a turning point, and falling action (like the plot in a story). Unlike many informational books, which we can open and read from any point to acquire the information we want, narrative nonfiction is best understood when it is read from beginning to end. Although text features like headings, visuals, and a table of contents can be found in both informational books and narrative nonfiction, the story-like structure that demands reading from start to finish is a key feature distinguishing a narrative nonfiction book from an informational book.

Narrative nonfiction books often center on contemporary or historical events told in a story form. For example, Larry Dane Brimner's *Twelve Days in May: Freedom Ride 1961* recounts the events of the May 1961 Freedom Ride from Washington, D.C., to New Orleans. Thirteen Black and White riders departed the nation's capital on buses to test whether Southern states adhered to the federal law prohibiting segregation on interstate transportation. The "characters" include the Freedom Riders such as James Farmer and John Lewis, and the day-by-day account of the Freedom Ride resembles a story plot. The action rises as the Freedom Riders travel further south and encounter increased hostilities, and the turning point occurs when two of the Freedom Ride buses are attacked by angry mobs in Birmingham and Anniston, Alabama. The action falls as the Freedom Riders arrive in New Orleans by plane and are greeted enthusiastically by civil rights supporters. The closing pages of the book are like an epilogue, sketching the lives of the original Freedom Riders following the events of May 1961.

Occasionally, narrative nonfiction books will include some features more often found in informational books. In *Spooked!: How a Radio Broadcast and The War of the Worlds Sparked the 1938 Invasion of America*, author Gail Jarrow relates how a radio broadcast of the H. G. Wells novel *The War of the Worlds* incited panic among some Americans. The presentation of the events is story-like and dramatic, very typical of what one would expect to find in narrative nonfiction. However, at the book's conclusion, the author shares information about hoaxes and describes several well-known hoaxes in American history. This section of the book is presented in an expository (rather than a narrative) fashion. However, the majority of the book is presented as a narrative, and therefore, it is best classified as narrative nonfiction. Recall from Chapter 2 that nonfiction books are not often strictly informational or strictly narrative but a hybrid of the two. It is the balance of informational to narrative text that helps us classify the subgenre of a nonfiction book.

Biographies and autobiographies are special forms of narrative nonfiction. Both are accounts of a person's life, but an autobiography is written by an author who tells about his, her, or their own life. *Becoming Kareem: Growing Up On and Off the Court* by basketball great Kareem Abdul-Jabbar is one example of a contemporary autobiography for middle-grade readers. Beginning from his childhood when he was known as Lew Alcindor, Abdul-Jabbar recounts his journey toward becoming his true self, including his growing awareness of prejudice, injustice, and civil right issues; success on the basketball court; conversion from Catholicism to Islam; and controversial name change. Memoirs are a type of autobiography. While autobiographies often cover most of the author's life span, a memoir tells a small slice of the author's life, such as his, her, or their role in a major event. *Turning 15 on the Road to Freedom* by Lynda Blackmon Lowery is one example. In this memoir, Lowery shares the story of her participation in the 1965 voting rights march that started in Selma, Alabama.

On the other hand, a biography is written by an author who tells about another person's life. For example, *Mama Africa*, written by Katherine Erskine and illustrated by Charly Palmer, is a picture book biography relating the life of Miriam Makeba, an acclaimed singer from South Africa who used her fame to advocate against the oppressive apartheid system in her home country. *Schomburg: The Man Who Built a Library* by Carole Boston Weatherford and illustrated by Eric Velasquez is a unique form of biography. Told as a series of free verse poems, Weatherford informs readers about the life and work of Arturo Schomburg, an Afro-Puerto Rican man dedicated to collecting books and artifacts celebrating Black achievements. Peppered throughout the account of Schomburg's life are brief biographical sketches of the Black heroes that Schomburg uncovered in his quest: Benjamin Banneker, Frederick Douglass, and Marcus Garvey, among others.

EVALUATING NARRATIVE NONFICTION

The evaluation criteria discussed in Chapter 2 also apply to narrative nonfiction. The credibility of the author remains important for narrative nonfiction as it is for informational books. Award-winning narrative nonfiction author Steve Sheinkin is especially known for presenting credible and trustworthy accounts of historical events. As he was writing *Undefeated: Jim Thorpe and the Carlisle Indian School Football Team*, Sheinkin consulted hundreds of newspaper articles dating from the early 1900s as well as ninety-seven books, articles, and websites to inform his narrative about one of the greatest football teams the sport has known. While Sheinkin is not a subject matter expert on the early days of college football, his extensive research, which included many primary sources, assures us of the authority of the facts he presents. Examining back matter such as the author's bibliography, sources, or works cited page can help us determine whether the book has credibility. In addition, accuracy matters when selecting narrative nonfiction. Educators and librarians should look for books suggesting the manuscript has been vetted by those knowledgeable about the content presented. For instance, Caren Stelson, author of *Sachiko: A Nagasaki Bomb Survivor's Story*, thanks numerous experts such as history and physics professors for helping her ensure the accuracy of her narrative.

Well-written narrative nonfiction should have a plot emphasizing main events relevant to the book's overall purpose. *Ruth Bader Ginsburg: The Case of R.B.G. vs. Inequality* is a picture book biography about the injustices faced by Ginsburg, one of the few women and Jewish Americans who have served on the U.S. Supreme Court. In keeping with the book's purpose of exposing gender and religious inequality, author Jonah Winter's narrative emphasizes events such as Ginsburg's experiences with anti-Semitism and gender discrimination in law school. Winter does not include every event in Ginsburg's long life and illustrious career—only the important ones given his purpose. We imagine many readers would lose interest in a cradle-to-grave biography with copious amounts of facts and details. Just like a good lesson plan should stick to its stated objectives, the plot of good narrative nonfiction should stick to its author's main purpose.

We have encountered children and even fellow teachers who complain that nonfiction is "dry" or "boring" to read. But nonfiction is far from boring. Just like the best works of fiction, excellent narrative nonfiction has captivating, page-turning writing and vivid visuals that enliven the subject. Author Candace Fleming is particularly gifted with her ability to transport readers into another time and place. In *The Family Romanov*, a biography of Russia's last royal family, Fleming describes the breathtaking moment when Empress Alexandra arrives at a lavish costume ball held at St. Petersburg's Winter Palace:

> Alexandra was wearing a gold brocade gown shimmering with the thousands of diamonds and pearls that had been sewn onto it—a costume that cost one million rubles ($10 million today). Her elaborate headdress glittered with diamonds and emeralds, and her pearl earrings were so heavy it was hard for her to hold up her head. Around her neck hung an enormous 400-carat blue sapphire. (p. 4)

Fleming's descriptive writing and precise words help us visualize Alexandra's opulent costume. Moreover, the photographs of the Romanov family appearing throughout the book satisfy our curiosity and enable us to understand the family's mind-boggling wealth.

When evaluating a biography, we should consider whether the author shares a balanced portrayal of the person's life. Everybody has flaws, even people who have made remarkable contributions to humankind. For example, in *Josephine: The Dazzling Life of Josephine Baker*, author Patricia Hruby Powell recounts an incredible life from Baker's early days living in poverty to her successful career as a dancer. There is much to admire about Baker, but Powell reminds us that she, like the rest of us, was imperfect, such as when Baker spends all of her money and faces eviction from her home. Well-written biographies should include the subject's flaws and follies. Authors of autobiographies should also be honest in portraying their lives. In *Becoming Kareem*, Abdul-Jabbar goes beyond describing his success as an athlete by relating the painful, trust-shattering experiences with racism he encountered as a young man. Young readers appreciate the inspiration that biographies and autobiographies provide (Hartsfield, 2017), and it is important for them to see that individuals do not need to be perfect to accomplish great things.

READING NARRATIVE NONFICTION WITH A CRITICAL LITERACY LENS

In Chapter 1, we explained that part of being a critically literate reader is recognizing that every text by every author has a bias. Consciously or not, authors are always attempting to position readers in some way. Even when a book is fact based, there is no such thing as neutrality. Paying special attention to whom and what authors choose to present and whom and what they choose to leave out can help us understand authors' bias and how authors want us (as readers) to be positioned. Looking carefully at *what* the author says and *how* the author says it—much like Jacob's students were doing in the opening vignette of this chapter—can help us understand the stance the author wants us to take. Questions like those in Sidebar 4.1 can help students unpack the author's positioning when reading narrative nonfiction.

Sidebar 4.1   Question Stems for Narrative Nonfiction

- What was the author's purpose in writing about this event or person? What themes does the author present?
- How does the author describe the people featured in the book? Who is described favorably? Who is described unfavorably?
- What events in the person's life are given prominence? Are there any key events in the person's life that the author left out? Why do you think the author highlighted some events and excluded others?
- Which events or people are accompanied by visuals? Which are not? What reasons could have influenced the author's decision to include visuals for some events or people and not others?
- What is the author's identity in terms of race, class, nationality, and so on? How might this identity influence the position the author takes?

We will illustrate our point here using Martin Sandler's *The Whydah*, which traces the history of a ship from the eighteenth century through the present day. The ship *Whydah* began its seafaring days as a slave vessel in the triangular trade route, but it was eventually captured by the notorious and fearsome pirate captain "Black Sam" Bellamy, who made it the flagship of his fleet. Bellamy lived outside the law, plundering countless other ships and developing a "ferocious" and "brutal" reputation (p. 11). Bellamy was a criminal who would have been executed for his crimes. So why do we cheer for him each time he triumphs? Why are we so devastated when the *Whydah* sinks and Bellamy perishes in the shipwreck?

It has much to do with the way Sandler presents him. We learn that Bellamy came from humble origins, and his clever and cunning nature catapulted him from unemployed sailor to treasure-laden pirate captain; he exemplified the rags-to-riches tales that Americans love so well. We learn that Bellamy may have been the tragic hero of an ill-fated romance, never able to return home to the woman he loved and intended to marry. We learn that Bellamy was nicknamed the "Robin Hood of the Seas," stealing the bounty of wealthy governments and companies and sharing it fairly with his men. We learn that Bellamy belonged to a pirate culture that was much more democratic and egalitarian than the socially and politically oppressive government he left behind. We learn these things, but we do not learn what cruel acts he may have facilitated. To understand how Sandler is positioning us (and to make ourselves aware of this positioning), we ask, "What is the author showing us? What is the author probably leaving out?"

Another example is Sandra Jordan and Jan Greenberg's picture book biography *Meet Cindy Sherman: Artist, Photographer, Chameleon*. The biography begins with Sherman's childhood and traces her journey through art school and her success as a photographer. Many of Sherman's important works from each decade of her life are presented. The authors tell us Sherman is a risk-taker who boldly captures the ambiguous, grotesque, and unusual, and they support this contention by showcasing Sherman's art throughout their book. They also include the voices of children who share their analyses of Sherman's photos. Clearly, the authors want us to appreciate Sherman as an artist, and their inclusion of children's voices suggests her work is accessible to everyone, even the youngest audience.

Yet Jordan and Greenberg say nothing about some of Sherman's most controversial and provocative works, namely her Busrider series, which depicts Sherman (a White woman) in Black face, and her Sex Parts series, which includes images of plastic mannequin parts juxtaposed in suggestive positions. Some might criticize these series for being racially insensitive and vulgar, respectively. The silence around these works is a deliberate choice; the book's bibliography shows that Jordan and Greenberg read a sizable number of sources about Sherman, and surely they were familiar with the different stages of her career. Why did the authors leave out these well-known series in Sherman's body of work? What do they want us to think about Sherman? By excluding these series from the book, we can speculate that the authors feel some topics are not appropriate for youth, or perhaps they want us to think that Sherman is a "safe" artist, one who pushed boundaries but was not overly risqué. Alternatively, we can speculate that the authors may have been worried about including controversial content in the book. By considering what has been left out of the book, we are challenging the authors and refusing to accept the stance they present to us.

An author's word choices can also reveal how we are being positioned and what biases the author has. In *Twelve Days in May*, we notice that each time Larry Dane Brimner introduces a person, he identifies the person's race. In this way, Brimner avoids the "white default" (Smith, 2016), the assumption that any character or person who is not racially identified must be White. Brimner is making a deliberate choice here. By naming race, we can speculate that Brimner does not think one race should be the "default," that one race is somehow so superior that it does not require mentioning. In this subtle way, Brimner is positioning Blacks and Whites as equals, and he wants us to think that too, which is in keeping with his book's themes of civil rights and striving for racial equality.

This topic of analyzing an author's word choices is the subject of our next chapter. Using *Andrew Jackson: The Making of America*, we explain how close reading can be used as a strategy for teaching students to develop a critical literacy stance when reading narrative nonfiction.

ANNOTATED BIBLIOGRAPHY

Abdul-Jabbar, Kareem, & Obstfeld, Raymond. *Becoming Kareem: Growing Up On and Off the Court*. 2017. 304 pp. Little, Brown Books for Young Readers. 9780316555388
Basketball great Kareem Abdul-Jabbar recalls his journey toward finding his true self beginning from his childhood years, including the mentors who shaped his identity and career.

Brimner, Larry Dane. *Twelve Days in May: Freedom Ride 1961*. 2017. 112 pp. Caulkins Creek. 9781629795867
Brimner presents a day-by-day account of the first Freedom Ride from Washington, D.C., to New Orleans by thirteen Black and White civil rights activists.

Erskine, Katherine. *Mama Africa!: How Miriam Makeba Spread Hope with Her Song.* Palmer, Charly. 2017. 48 pp. Farrar, Straus and Giroux. 9780374303013
This biography shares the life of Miriam Makeba, a South African singer who used her fame to call attention to the oppressive apartheid system in her home country.

Fleming, Candace. *The Family Romanov: Murder, Rebellion, and the Fall of Imperial Russia.* 2014. 304 pp. Schwartz & Wade. 9780375867828
Gripping and dramatic, this biography presents the final years of Nicholas II, the last tzar of Russia, and his callous treatment of his subjects that ultimately led to revolution and his demise.

Freedman, Russell. *We Will Not Be Silent: The White Rose Student Resistance Movement That Defied Adolf Hitler.* 2016. 112 pp. Clarion Books. 9780544223790
Not all Germans were willing to accept the atrocities of Hitler and the Nazi regime. Teen siblings Hans and Sophie Scholl and their friends were among those brave enough to speak out. This book chronicles their involvement in the White Rose Student Resistance Movement and untimely deaths.

Greenberg, Jan, & Jordan, Sandra. *Meet Cindy Sherman: Artist, Photographer, Chameleon.* 2017. 64 pp. Roaring Brook Press. 9781626725201
This biography explains the life and artistic process of Cindy Sherman, a photographer known for her boundary-breaking work.

Jarrow, Gail. *Spooked!: How a Radio Broadcast and The War of the Worlds Sparked the 1938 Invasion of America.* 2018. 144 pp. Calkins Creek. 978162797762
On Halloween eve in 1938, a radio performance of the H. G. Wells novel *The War of the Worlds* by Orson Welles and the Mercury Theatre group incited panic among Americans who believed the alien invasion reported in the broadcast was real. Readers are invited to consider the impact of "fake news" and the importance of critically evaluating the media.

Kanefield, Teri. *Andrew Jackson: The Making of America.* 2018. 243 pp. Abrams Books for Young Readers. 9781419728402
Major events in the life of Andrew Jackson are detailed in this biography, including his cruel and oppressive policies toward Native Americans and people of color.

Lowery, Lynda Blackmon, Leacock, Elspeth, & Buckley, Susan. *Turning 15 on the Road to Freedom: My Story of the 1965 Selma Voting Rights March.* 2015. 144 pp. Speak. 9780147512161
In this memoir, Lynda Blackmon Lowery recalls her experiences in the 1965 Voting Rights March from Selma to Montgomery.

Powell, Patricia Hruby. *Josephine: The Dazzling Life of Josephine Baker.* Robinson, Christian. 2014. 104 pp. Chronicle Books. 9781452103143
This poetic biography reveals Josephine Baker's remarkable life from her impoverished childhood in St. Louis to her fame as an acclaimed dancer.

Sandler, Martin W. *The Whydah: A Pirate Ship Feared, Wrecked, and Found.* 2017. 176 pp. Candlewick. 9780763680336
This book follows the history of the Whydah, a former slave vessel captained by Sam Bellamy that became the first treasure-laden pirate ship ever excavated.

Sheinkin, Steve. *Undefeated: Jim Thorpe and the Carlisle Indian School Football Team.* 2017. 288 pp. Roaring Brook Press. 9781596439542
Undefeated traces the history of football, including the innovations by the remarkable Carlisle Indian School team and Jim Thorpe, considered to be one of the world's greatest athletes.

Stelson, Caren. *Sachiko: A Nagasaki Bomb Survivor's Story.* 2016. 144 pp. Carolrhoda Books. 9781467789035
This biography recounts the life and experiences of Sachiko Yasui, a survivor of the 1945 bombing of Nagasaki, Japan, by the United States.

Weatherford, Carole Boston. *Schomburg: The Man Who Built a Library.* Velasquez, Eric. 2017. 48 pp. Candlewick. 9780763680466
Told in poetic verse, this biography shares the life of Arturo Schomburg, who devoted his life to collecting artifacts showcasing the achievements of the African diaspora.
Winter, Jonah. *Ruth Bader Ginsburg: The Case of R.B.G. vs. Inequality.* Innerest, Stacey. 2017. 48 pp. Harry N. Abrams. 9781419725593
Presented as a court case where readers act as the jury, this biography describes the challenges faced and met by Ruth Bader Ginsburg, the second female to serve on the U.S. Supreme Court.

5

Close Reading and Analyzing Word Choice in Narrative Nonfiction (Lesson Plan)

As we explained in Chapter 1, those who embrace a critical literacy stance assume that no text is ever neutral. Even when a text is reporting "just the facts," the text always reflects the author's bias. As readers, we can make ourselves aware of this bias by considering what information the author chooses to include in the text and how the author frames this information. Close reading is a strategy that can help students gain a deep understanding of the text and how it is structured (Fisher & Frey, 2014). Although proficient readers have long used this strategy to interpret the meaning of a text, it has become more widely used as a result of the Common Core State Standards (National Governors Association Center for Best Practices & Council of Chief State School Officers, 2010) and the emphasis on teaching students to justify their thinking using text-based evidence. Though close reading is intended to promote students' comprehension, it can also help students unpack author bias and develop their stance as critically literate readers.

According to Fisher and Frey (2014), close reading involves multiple steps on the part of the teacher and students. First, the teacher must select a text suitable for close reading. The text should be challenging for students, and it must lend itself to critical analysis because students will read the text beyond the surface or literal level. Second, students read the text multiple times. With each reading, the students read with a different question or focus in mind. For example, the first time students read a text, they might read for the purpose of understanding the text's main idea or message. In subsequent readings, they read in response to a particular question. All questions for close reading should be developed by the teacher prior to the lesson and relate to the lesson objectives and the teacher's purpose for assigning the text. As students read, they are responsible for locating evidence in the text that supports the answer to the question; they often annotate the text by making notes, highlighting, underlining, or circling so they may quickly return to key information that supports their thinking. When students are learning how to use the close reading strategy, they benefit from scaffolding by the teacher. The teacher should model the process for close reading and use "think-alouds" to show students how proficient readers locate and interpret textual evidence. Finally, students should be given opportunities to respond to the text. They may participate in a discussion with peers or construct a written response. No matter how students respond, it is important for students to ground their thinking using specific textual evidence.

In the remainder of this chapter, we return to Jacob's sixth-grade classroom. The students are learning about the antebellum period of American history, and they are about to study the presidency of Andrew Jackson. Jacob recognizes that Jackson's controversial presidency and complex personality could make excellent opportunities for helping his students become critically literate readers. He decides to assign his students to read the prologue of *Andrew Jackson: The Making of America*, a biography by Teri Kanefield. They will use the close reading strategy to analyze how Kanefield portrays Jackson in the opening pages of the book; they will carefully examine her word choices and the way she describes Jackson and his supporters. In this lesson, students learn content about Andrew Jackson. They also learn that authors position readers in a certain way through the choices they make in their writing, but active and critical reading can help readers be aware of what the author wants them to think. Now, we turn to the lesson that Jacob will teach his students (Table 5.1).

Table 5.1   Lesson Plan

Central focus: Students will *analyze* the word choices and information presented in a text to determine the author's stance.	**Subject:** English language arts and social studies
Grade: 6	**Classroom context:** Whole group

Standards

CCSS.ELA-LITERACY.RI.6.1: Cite textual evidence to support analysis of what the text says explicitly as well as inferences drawn from the text.
CCSS.ELA-LITERACY.RI.6.6: Determine an author's point of view or purpose in a text and explain how it is conveyed in the text.

Objectives

Students will *know* that the information and word choices included in a text can reveal the author's stance toward the topic.

Students will *understand* that careful, close reading of text can reveal an author's biases.

Students will *be able to* identify the author's stance in a text by analyzing the word choices and information presented.

Assessment: At the end of this lesson, students will write a short response in their social studies notebooks. Their responses should explain what they think the author believes about Andrew Jackson and his supporters and what evidence in the text makes them think this. The teacher will collect students' responses and review them to determine if students have constructed a reasonable interpretation of the author's stance supported by at least three pieces of evidence from the text. In addition, the teacher will informally assess students through questioning and observation throughout the lesson; the teacher will be listening and watching to see if students are noticing word choices and describing information that helps them interpret the author's stance.

Materials

Copies of the prologue (pp. 1–4) of *Andrew Jackson: The Making of America* by Teri Kanefield (one copy for each student)

Images of a young man "looting" and a couple "finding food" during Hurricane Katrina to be displayed for students (see http://www.lookingglassnews.org/viewstory.php?storyid=2304)

Academic language function: Analyze	**Language demands:** Reading a text, writing a response to a text, speaking in response to a text, listening to peers respond to a text

Lesson introduction

1. The teacher displays the image of a young man "looting" in the aftermath of Hurricane Katrina. The teacher asks students to take a few minutes to read the photo's caption carefully. The caption says: "A young man walks through chest deep flood water after looting a grocery store in New Orleans on Tuesday, Aug. 30, 2005."

2. Then, the teacher asks students what they think about the young man in the picture after reading the caption. The teacher calls on a few students to share responses.

3. The teacher displays the image of a couple "finding" food and asks students to read the photo's caption carefully. The caption says: "Two residents wade through chest-deep water after finding bread and soda from a local grocery store after Hurricane Katrina came through the area in New Orleans."

4. The teacher asks students what they think about the couple in the picture after reading the caption. The teacher calls on a few students to share responses.

5. The teacher then displays both captions and images side by side. The teacher says: "Both photos show people who gathered food after Hurricane Katrina, a natural disaster that devastated the Gulf coast region and left many people homeless. How were your reactions to these two photos similar and different? If your reactions were different, why do you think they were different? Think for a minute, then share with a neighbor." Students turn and talk about the photos and their reactions.

6. After allotting several minutes for students to talk to peers, the teacher calls for the attention of the whole class and asks for several students to compare and contrast their reactions and the reasons for their reactions. As students share, they may realize that the photo of the young man may be perceived more negatively because he is "looting," while the couple may be perceived more positively because they are "finding food." (If students do not notice this, the teacher may need to do a think-aloud to bring it to the attention of students.)

7. The teacher says, "We don't know what happened before the photos were taken, but we can guess that both the young man and the couple found food wherever they could because the city was flooded and stores were closed. Some people might see the young man as a criminal because he is 'looting,' and some people might see the couple as victims of a hurricane because they are

(Continued)

Table 5.1   Lesson Plan (Continued)

'finding food.' We are not learning about Hurricane Katrina in today's lesson, but I wanted you to see these photos and their captions because they are a well-known example of how word choices can shape our opinions and reveal the bias, or the opinion, of the writer. We might assume that the person who wrote the caption about the young man thought it was wrong for him to take food from the grocery store without permission; the word 'looting' suggests this. And we might assume that the person who wrote the caption about the couple was feeling sympathetic toward them; the phrase 'finding food' does not imply that they did something wrong like the word 'looting' does. Word choices are powerful, and authors select words intentionally to convey a message. If we are careful readers, we can often tell what an author thinks by closely examining what words the author selects and the information that the author chooses to present."

8. The teacher explains the purpose of the lesson: "Today, we are starting a new unit in social studies about Andrew Jackson, the seventh president of the United States, and we are going to read parts of a book called *Andrew Jackson: The Making of America*. In this lesson, we will learn how to use a strategy called close reading to determine what the author of this book thinks about Andrew Jackson. Learning how to be a close reader is an important skill. If you are aware of the author's bias when you read something, then you don't have to accept what the author is telling you. You can challenge what the author says and decide whether you agree or disagree with what the author is saying."

Instructional input/teacher modeling

9. The teacher distributes copies of the prologue from *Andrew Jackson: The Making of America*. "We are going to read about Andrew Jackson's first inauguration in this prologue; it will tell us about the day he became the president of the United States. Please read the first two paragraphs silently. Read to determine the main ideas in these two paragraphs. Look up to let me know when you are done."

10. After giving students a few minutes to read, the teacher says, "The main idea of these two paragraphs is that many people attended the inauguration of Andrew Jackson, the seventh president of the United States."

11. The teacher says, "When we do close reading, we read the text multiple times. Each time we read the text, we deepen our understanding of the text's meaning. We are going to read these two paragraphs again. This time, I want you to think about how the author feels about Andrew Jackson as you read. What does she want us to think about him? Take your time reading, and look up when you are done." Students begin reading silently.

12. After students have read the text a second time, the teacher begins to model how close reading can help students understand what the author thinks. The first two paragraphs of the prologue are displayed on the board, and the teacher reads the first paragraph aloud. The teacher then says: "Some of the things the author says in this first paragraph give me clues about what she thinks about Andrew Jackson. First, I wonder about the title of the prologue: *A Mob in the White House*." The teacher underlines "mob" on the board. "I think the word 'mob' is an interesting choice by the author; when I hear 'mob,' it makes me

think of a large group of people who are misbehaving or making trouble. The author could have used the word 'crowd' instead, but she chose 'mob.' I think the author believes the people who came to see Andrew Jackson's inauguration were wild and unruly. I also wonder about the words the author uses to describe Andrew Jackson. She says he has 'piercing blue eyes' that 'radiated strength and vitality.'" The teacher stops and underlines these phrases on the board. "I can infer that the author thinks Jackson was a powerful man based on this description. She could have just said that Jackson had blue eyes, but she chooses words like 'strength' and 'vitality' to make Jackson seem like a commanding person. The author also tells us that Jackson 'carried two bullets lodged in his body' from participating in 'frontier gunfights and his own hot temper.'" The teacher underlines the phrases on the board. "If we were in the crowd watching Jackson's inauguration, we would not see those bullets or know they were there. But the author tells us about them in the very first paragraph! The author must think this reveals something significant about Jackson. She tells us the bullets come from gunfights and Jackson's bad temper. By telling us this, the author probably wants us to think that Jackson was a wild and unruly person, much like the mob of people who came to see his inauguration."

13. Next, the teacher reads aloud the second paragraph, underlining the phrase "a man from the backcountry." The teacher says, "I think this phrase is significant, too. The author could have said Jackson lived much of his life in Tennessee, but instead she says 'backcountry,' which means a very rural area that doesn't have many people. Maybe the author was trying to be more descriptive by using 'backcountry,' but it's also possible that the author wants us to think that Jackson was uncivilized because he grew up in such a remote area."

14. The teacher says, "As I just modeled, I read the text to myself multiple times, and after the first time, I underlined words, phrases, and information that suggested what the author might think. As I read, I thought about what the author *could have said* and compared it to what the author *actually said*; this helped me decide what the author might think. After reading these two paragraphs, I think the author believes Jackson was a powerful man who was unruly and perhaps a bit wild, and analyzing the word choices in the text helped me decide this. Now that I know this bias, I understand what the author is trying to make me think, and I can decide if I want to accept or reject what the author says."

Work session

15. "Now we are going to try close reading together. Please read the next four paragraphs silently to yourself. When you are done, talk with the people at your table group about the main idea and key details in these four paragraphs." The teacher gives the students several minutes to read and discuss the assigned paragraphs. The teacher calls on one or two groups to share the main ideas and key details with the whole class.

(*Continued*)

Table 5.1   Lesson Plan (Continued)

16. The teacher says, "Please read the four paragraphs again. This time, you should read with these questions in mind: *What does the author want us to think about Andrew Jackson? What does the author want us to think about the people who attended Jackson's inauguration?* (The teacher writes these questions on the board to help students remember them.) Underline key phrases that help you decide what the author wants you to think. When everyone at your table is done reading, talk together about what you noticed."

17. After students have had several minutes to reread the text and talk about the focus questions, the teacher asks each group to share what they discussed with the whole class. As students respond, the teacher encourages them to refer back to the text and point out specific things the author says. The paragraphs students read in Step 16 shift into Jackson's behavior on his inauguration day and the way he tried to present himself to the public. Students might notice the following: "servant of the people" paints Jackson as a common man, not an elite; "humbly noted" conveys the author's belief that Jackson was trying to appear modest; "the crowd lunged" and "the crowd . . . swarmed" imply the unruliness of Jackson's admirers; and "defying custom" suggests the author wants readers to think that Jackson was different from previous presidents. If students do not notice these phrases in the text, the teacher may do a think-aloud to help students understand what the author wants readers to think about Jackson. However, the teacher accepts a range of interpretations as long as students support their ideas using the text.

18. After discussing the text as a whole class, the teacher summarizes the ideas that have been shared so far: "The author wants us to think that Jackson is a powerful, strong man because he has piercing eyes and bullets in his body. But additionally, she might want us to think that Jackson is a common person, an ordinary man who became president, and she does this by telling us about his humble behavior and defiance of presidential tradition. She highlights this portrayal by also telling us that Jackson's admirers were a disorderly group of people. By presenting these two characterizations in the same text—Jackson the powerful and Jackson the common man—the author might want us to think that perhaps Jackson was also a bit deceptive. He acted one way in private and a different way when he was in public. What do you think about that? Why would Jackson behave that way?" The teacher calls on several students to share their thinking.

19. The teacher tells students, "Let's see if our analysis of the author's portrayal of Andrew Jackson remains true as we continue reading the prologue. Maybe we will change our minds about what the author is trying to get us to think if we read further and learn more information. Now you are going to practice close reading on your own. First, read the remainder of the prologue silently to yourself. When you finish reading, think about the main ideas of these remaining paragraphs. Next, reread these paragraphs again with these focus questions in mind: *What does the author want us to think about Andrew Jackson? What does the author want us to think about the people who attended Jackson's inauguration?* Underline important words and phrases that you can use to justify your thinking as you read. When you are done reading, take out your social studies notebook. Write a response explaining what the author

wants you, the reader, to think about Andrew Jackson and his admirers in the prologue to this book. Make sure that you use at least three pieces of evidence from the prologue to support what you think."

20. The students begin working independently. They read the remainder of the prologue and write their responses in their notebooks.

Lesson closure

21. After the students have had sufficient time to work, the teacher calls on several students to share their writing with the class. The teacher asks the class if they have similar or different responses than the students who shared their writing.

22. The teacher asks, "We talked about some of the ways that the author characterized Andrew Jackson. We understand what she is trying to make us think about our seventh president. Why do you think the author wants us to think this way? In other words, what could be the author's reasons for portraying Jackson in this way? Turn and talk to a friend for a few minutes, and then we will share our thinking with everyone." The teacher will call on some students to share; responses may vary. The teacher should make note of what students say and return to their ideas later in the unit when students know more about Andrew Jackson and his policies.

23. During the last few minutes of the lesson, the teacher asks students to consider what they learned about Andrew Jackson in the lesson and make predictions about what policies and legislation Jackson might have favored while he was president. Students write their predictions in their social studies notebooks, and the teacher collects them for assessment as the lesson ends.

Differentiation

Some students may require extra support during this lesson. For students who struggle with reading, the teacher might read the text aloud or provide the students with an audio recording. Students who are not ready to move on to independent practice could work with the teacher in a small group similar to the steps in the guided practice part of the lesson.

Students who need a challenge could be asked to rewrite a portion of the prologue. Students write about the event featured in the prologue (Andrew Jackson's inauguration day) using facts stated in the text, but they are asked to characterize Jackson differently than the author by choosing alternate ways of describing Jackson.

MODIFYING THE LESSON PLAN

Of course, not everyone reading this book will teach a sixth-grade history lesson just like Jacob's. The strategy we have described in this lesson can be applied in other classroom contexts. In the fourth and fifth grades, teachers could teach this strategy by increasing the level of teacher scaffolding. For example, instead of students selecting phrases that describe Andrew Jackson as in Steps 16 and 19 of this lesson plan, the teacher could choose phrases that reveal the author's characterization of Jackson in advance. The teacher could share these phrases with students, and after careful modeling by the teacher, the teacher and students could work together to analyze the author's purpose for including these phrases in the text. In the seventh and eighth grades, students could compare Kanefield's account of Jackson's inauguration with other written accounts. Students could closely read both texts to examine the different ways that the authors characterize Jackson. This is in line with Standard 6 of the Reading Informational Text strand of the Common Core State Standards in English Language Arts (National Governors Association Center for Best Practices & Council of Chief State School Officers, 2010). In addition, students could read selections of the sources Kanefield used to construct her narrative of Jackson's inauguration and decide if Kanefield herself was creating her account using text-based evidence from her sources. This activity could help students understand that authors are selective in what they choose to present to readers. In addition, teachers can modify this lesson by selecting a different text that is suitable to their students' instructional needs and their curricular goals. However, teachers should remember that the text they select for close reading should be challenging.

6

Historical Fiction

We can hear the noise coming from Robert's fifth-grade English language arts/ social studies class moments before we arrive at the classroom door. Multiple students are talking at once, their voices rising and falling in the depths of a conversation. What is the reason for all of this noise? Has Robert lost control of his class? Are his classroom management skills slipping?

Not at all. As we enter the classroom, we see students arranged in two circles: one inner circle and one outer circle. The students in the inner circle are facing a partner in the outer circle; one partner speaks while the other listens. The students in the class are studying antebellum Americans' attitudes about slavery, and they have recently read two novels, The Journey of Little Charlie *and* Martha and the Slave Catchers, *as part of their unit. Robert intentionally paired these novels for this unit. Both are works of historical fiction that yield insights into how different groups of Americans, particularly White Americans, in the mid-1800s thought about slavery and enslaved people. Robert is using the concentric circles approach (Gonzalez, 2015) to structure and facilitate students' discussion about why different groups of people held different views of slavery. The loudness of Robert's classroom is no accident—it is a sign of students engaged in thoughtful learning and making connections across texts. In Chapter 7, we will explore how pairing texts can be used as a critical literacy strategy for understanding multiple perspectives. In the meantime, we discuss the genre of historical fiction and explore how it can assist students with developing a critical literacy perspective.*

DEFINING HISTORICAL FICTION

Historical fiction books feature realistic and plausible characters, settings, and situations. As the name of the genre suggests, works of historical fiction are set in the past. What constitutes "the past" has no simple definition. Books set during the American Revolution, the Civil War, or the Industrial Revolution are clearly historical fiction; no person who experienced these events is alive now. Although we suspect that many contemporary adults would prefer not to think of the 1960s, 1970s, 1980s, or even 1990s as "historic" times, these decades may seem radically different to many children in the present. For the purpose of this book, we consider books set in the year 2000 or later as contemporary realistic fiction and books set in the 1990s and earlier as historical fiction. The turn of the millennium provides a convenient marker for distinguishing contemporary from historic times; the year 2000 predates the birth of today's middle-grade students, and books set before this time would seem like the distant past to these learners.

Historical fiction books for children are often set against the backdrop of actual events and places. For example, *The Island at the End of Everything* is set on Culion, an island in the Philippines that was once the largest colony in the world for people with Hansen's disease (leprosy). *The War That Saved My Life* and its sequel, *The War I Finally Won*, both take place in the United Kingdom during World War II, and *Memphis, Martin, and the Mountaintop* is set during the Memphis sanitation workers' strike of 1968. In other books, the settings and events are entirely imagined by the author. The fictitious small town of Rainbow, Georgia, is the setting of *Walking with Miss Millie*. However, the story still reflects the racial tensions between Blacks and Whites that one might have encountered in the rural Deep South of the 1960s.

Real people from the past may also appear in historical fiction, though this is not a requirement of books belonging to the genre. In *Al Capone Throws Me a Curve*, the titular character makes a minor appearance (as he does in several other titles within this four-part series). Katy, the protagonist of *Out of Left Field*, has an opportunity to play baseball with the legendary Willie Mays as the Giants began their inaugural year in San Francisco. Sometimes the real people in historical fiction are famous (such as Al Capone and Willie Mays), but in other books, authors present the lives of lesser-known individuals. *River Runs Deep* is about a boy, Elias, who is sent to an experimental hospital located in Kentucky's Mammoth Cave as a cure for his tuberculosis (or consumption, as it was called in the book's 1840s setting). While Elias was not a real person, Dr. John Crogan, a physician and owner of the cave, and Stephen Bishop, Nick Bransford, and Mat Bransford, enslaved men who helped others seek refuge in the cave, were all real people.

Some authors of historical fiction base their narratives on events in their own lives. For example, *Lucky Broken Girl* is about Ruthie, a Cuban immigrant living in New York City, who spends a year in a body cast as a result of a tragic car accident. The story is a fictionalized version of author Ruth Behar's own childhood experiences in the 1960s. Likewise, in *My Year in the Middle*, Lu is a sixth grader growing up in small-town Alabama during George Wallace's 1970 campaign for governor. As an Argentinian immigrant, Lu finds herself caught in the middle between her White friends, whom she seems to have less in common with than she once did, and her Black peers at her newly integrated school who share her interest in and talent for running track. *My Year in the Middle* is inspired by author Lila Quintero Weaver's own experiences during her adolescent years.

Reading historical fiction has many benefits to children. Historical fiction humanizes the people of the past to readers of the present day and gives children a reference point when learning about events in history. For instance, in schools today, children learn about the segregation and racial injustices that permeated life throughout much of the twentieth century in the United States. Young people are better positioned to understand what segregation was like when they can vicariously experience it through the lens of a character like Stella, an African American girl living in rural North Carolina during the early 1930s, in *Stella by Starlight*. Segregation and racial discrimination seem much less abstract when readers can see how it impacts the everyday experiences of Stella's family. Although reading a book can never fully teach children what it was like to live in earlier times, historical fiction can promote empathy for the people of the past and build children's schema of history.

Historical fiction can also introduce children to little-known events. While much has been written about escaping from slavery and the Underground Railroad, *Calico Girl* highlights a historical anecdote with which readers may not be familiar. As the Civil War began, Fort Monroe, a Union stronghold in Virginia, welcomed enslaved people who sought freedom. When news of Fort Monroe spread, many individuals fled slavery and found a safe haven at the fort. While the Fugitive Slave Act would have required the Union soldiers to return these individuals to their masters, Virginia was now a foreign country, no longer a part of the Union, and therefore not subject to the laws of the United States. Children may not encounter the intriguing story of Fort Monroe without a book like *Calico Girl*. Likewise, *The Edelweiss Pirates* shares a story of a young boy, Kurt, living in Germany under Adolf Hitler. Kurt longs to be like his older brother Albert, who leaves home each night to engage in covert activities: sometimes playing forbidden American jazz music and sometimes defacing swastika symbols in public places. As the author's note reveals, the Edelweiss Pirates was a real group comprising young people who resisted Hitler during the Nazi regime. Many children who learn about World War II and the Holocaust in school may be unfamiliar with the Edelweiss Pirates, and the book helps them understand that not all Germans were passive and accepting of Hitler's racist and xenophobic decrees. *What the Night Sings*, set during the aftermath of the Holocaust, also offers a glimpse into an unfamiliar side of history. Young people of today know that millions of people lost their lives in concentration camps, but what happened to the survivors after the war ended? Readers can find out by reading the story of Gerta, a teen who survives the Holocaust and migrates to Israel to start a new life. Historical fiction books make the past much more vivid and intriguing compared to what readers confront in their history textbooks at school.

Moreover, historical fiction can offer readers perspectives that they would be unlikely to see in the social studies and history textbooks they read in school. When we think about the 1950s, we tend to think of a relatively peaceful and prosperous decade sandwiched between the turmoil of the World War II years and the civil rights struggles of the 1960s. Television shows that children may still see in syndication today, such as *Happy Days*, contribute to this perception. However, the 1950s was not an idyllic time for all. This was still an oppressive period for women and girls as readers learn in *Out of Left Field*. In this novel, Katy Gordon is a fifth grader who is an ace on her neighborhood pitching mound. When she is scouted by a Little League coach, Katy tries out and makes the team. However, she is banned from playing when Little League authorities learn that she is a female. Despite Katy's talents and her efforts to convince officials otherwise, she is not allowed to play on a Little League team. Katy's point of view as a female facing gender discrimination in sports is not one that readers are likely to see when learning about the 1950s in school. In this way, Katy's story disrupts the typical narrative associated with life in the 1950s.

EVALUATING HISTORICAL FICTION

Because historical fiction is set during a time that may be unfamiliar to children, it is important for books in this genre to include a realistic and relatable protagonist. Langston, the protagonist of *Finding Langston*, is a strong example of this. The story is set in 1946, and Langston and his father have recently moved to Chicago from Alabama following the death of Langston's mother. While children may have little knowledge of American life in the immediate aftermath of World War II, they might relate to Langston's pain and raw grief at the loss of his mother; his struggles with fitting in at his new school, avoiding bullies, and making friends; and the joy and peace he finds in visiting the public library. Langston seems very real although his story takes place more than seventy years ago. We may see ourselves or someone we know reflected in his character, and this is true of nearly all quality historical fiction. Readers may not connect to historical fiction if they cannot reach across time and place to see something of themselves reflected in the story.

Historical fiction should reflect the values and norms of people who lived during the time period in which the story is set, yet characters may not necessarily conform (or want to conform) to these norms. In *Refugee*, Josef's Jewish family escapes from Nazi Germany by purchasing passage on a ship bound for Cuba. Although some Germans at that time openly discriminated against Jewish people, Captain Schroeder shows kindness to Josef and his family and the other Jewish passengers aboard the ship. However, the open hostility toward Jewish people is reflected in the character of Otto Schiendick, a crew member allegiant to the Nazi Party who takes every opportunity to harass Jewish people. Similarly, in *Beyond the Bright Sea*, protagonist Crow encounters prejudicial attitudes toward the people of Pekinese. A small island off the Massachusetts coast, Pekinese was once home to a leper hospital, and in the early twentieth century when this book is set, people feared and dreaded leprosy and avoided contact with the afflicted at all costs. Contrary to the attitudes of her neighbors and acquaintances, Crow, her guardian Osh, and her friend Miss Maggie empathize with the people who once populated Pekinese.

Historical fiction may include speech and language typical of the book's time period or of the characters' cultures. For example, Martha's mother in *Martha and the Slave Catchers* is a Quaker, and all of her dialogue is written according to the conventions of Quaker Plain Speech. If archaic speech patterns are used in a character's dialogue, they should not be excessive. Readers will lose interest if they feel they have to translate every line of the character's dialogue. Moreover, historical fiction should not include terminology or expressions that were nonexistent during the book's chronological setting. For instance, the term "adulting" has become popular in recent years to describe the challenges of "grown-up" tasks such as supporting oneself financially. The appearance of a modern term like "adulting" in a historical fiction book would suggest that the author did limited research about the time period. Although historical fiction is *fiction*, readers can still use these books as an opportunity to learn about life in the past. Anachronisms do not have a place in historical fiction.

Speaking of research, when evaluating historical fiction, read the author's note to determine if the author has consulted sources about the people, places, norms, and customs of the time period. Some authors will even include bibliographies. In the backmatter of *River Runs Deep*, author Jennifer Bradbury recommends a number of sources that she read when researching her book and explains what readers can expect to learn from each of them. Of course, authors of historical fiction are expected to add fictional elements to the people and events in their stories, but these fictional elements should be plausible for the time period.

Sometimes readers may encounter books that seem like nonfiction but would be better classified as historical fiction. For example, *Memphis, Martin, and the Mountaintop* appears to be a work of narrative nonfiction relating the 1968 Memphis sanitation workers' strike and the death of Dr. Martin Luther King Jr. The book does contain facts about these events, but it includes the perspective of Lorraine Jackson, a fictitious narrator, as well as details about the involvement of Lorraine's family in the strike. At a glance, this title seems like it is a nonfiction book. While it can be valuable for teaching children about history, readers must understand that this is a historical fiction book because the author has taken liberties with the facts. Educators are advised to read the author's note to determine if a book is nonfiction or historical fiction. The presence of a bibliography alone does not mean a book is nonfiction; as we discussed in the preceding paragraph, authors of historical fiction sometimes include a bibliography to demonstrate the credibility of their historical settings.

Special consideration should be given when evaluating historical fiction books featuring characters who are racial or ethnic minorities. Unfortunately, open discrimination against certain groups was a sad reality in the American past (and still is today). It is common for minority characters in historical fiction to face prejudice because this reflects the historical reality. However, minority characters should not always be portrayed as passive and helpless victims. Stephen in *River Runs Deep* protects fellow enslaved people making their way to freedom in the North. Stella's father in *Stella by Starlight* registers to vote despite facing threats and hostility. Lorraine and her family protest against unfair wages and working conditions in *Memphis, Martin, and the Mountaintop*. Characters who demonstrate agency in the face of injustice show children that there have always been people willing to take a stand even when justice was slow to come.

There are several awards that educators can consult when selecting quality historical fiction. The Scott O'Dell Award, named after noted children's author Scott O'Dell (perhaps most famous for *Island of the Blue Dolphins* and *Julie of the Wolves*), is given annually to outstanding works of historical fiction. The Notable Social Studies Tradebooks for Young People, a booklist compiled annually by the National Council for Social Studies, is another source for locating titles. While books do not have to belong to a specific genre to receive this award, works of historical fiction are often included on each year's list. Table 6.1 indicates where educators can look online for these awards.

Table 6.1   Sources for Selecting Historical Fiction

Award	Website
National Council for Social Studies Notable Social Studies Tradebooks for Young People	https://www.socialstudies.org/publications/notables#previous
Scott O'Dell Award	https://scottodell.com/the-scott-odell-award

READING HISTORICAL FICTION WITH A CRITICAL LITERACY LENS

Historical fiction lends itself especially well to developing a critical literacy stance. Through reading this genre, children can understand that many of the social justice issues we face today have been ongoing for many years. Today's children may be aware of racial issues such as police brutality against African Americans, the overrepresentation of people of color in prisons, and prejudicial attitudes against immigrants. Many works of historical fiction depict discrimination against various groups of people, including *Walking with Miss Millie*, *Stella by Starlight*, *The Journey of Little Charlie*, *Martha and the Slave Catchers*, and *My Year in the Middle*. When children understand that these problems have existed before their lifetimes and yet still persist today, children are prompted to wonder "Why is that?" and "What can I do to make things better?" Such critical questioning and action-taking are the heart of critical literacy.

In our experience with reading historical fiction, we have noticed that many protagonists in these books develop a critical literacy perspective through their encounters with injustice. These characters can serve as an example of enacting critical literacy to readers:

- In *The Edelweiss Pirates*, Kurt observes the mistreatment of his Jewish friend Fritz at school and becomes ashamed of himself for doing nothing. Kurt decides to take action and stand up against discriminatory Nazi policies by playing forbidden American jazz music at the school concert.

- Elias in *River Runs Deep* and Charlie in *The Journey of Little Charlie* are both White children who, despite initial attitudes of prejudice and White supremacy, begin to respect Black people and view them as fellow human beings rather than "property" or second-class citizens. Both take action to assist the Black characters they have come to respect and admire. Elias assists in an effort to maintain the secrecy of a refuge for runaway enslaved people, and Little Charlie helps prevent a free Black youth from being seized by a slave catcher.

- Katy in *Out of Left Field* exercises critical literacy through taking action against the discriminatory policies of Little League, which does not allow female players. Katy writes a persuasive letter to Little League, and when her request is turned down, she begins her quest to undermine the argument that women do not play baseball.

Sidebar 6.1   Question Stems for Historical Fiction

- Why might the author have decided to write about this time period?
- What attitudes and beliefs might the author have toward the historical events and issues presented in this book?
- What social justice issues are present in this book? Why did the author include them? How do these relate to social justice issues in today's world?
- From whose perspective is the story told? Is this perspective underrepresented or overrepresented in stories and historical texts about this time period? Whose interests are served by telling the story from this perspective?

- Lu in *My Year in the Middle* questions the racial divide among her peers at school. Despite the controversy she knows it will cause, she eventually rejects her White friends who exhibit prejudicial attitudes and befriends Black classmates who treat her kindly and share her interests.

When educators wish to show students what enacting critical literacy could look like, they can point to these examples. Although fictional, they present realistic situations of young people taking actions against injustice.

A strategy that we recommend when reading historical fiction is pairing texts. When texts sharing similar themes are paired, students can see that history comprises multiple perspectives, and this enriches their understanding of the social and political issues presented. For example, in the next chapter, we describe a lesson in which *The Journey of Little Charlie* is paired with *Martha and the Slave Catchers* to show students the varying attitudes and beliefs that different groups of people had toward slavery. In these two books, students encounter the perspectives of an impoverished Southern sharecropping family; a staunchly abolitionist family in Connecticut that assists with the Underground Railroad; slave catchers charged with capturing runaways; and a wealthy plantation owner. Although we hope that today's readers would condemn slavery and recognize it as a shameful part of the American past, reading both of these books and being exposed to these different perspectives can help students understand why slavery was a divisive and contentious issue in the mid-1800s. While it can be uncomfortable to read about the racist perspectives of plantation owners and slave catchers, especially when we recognize the inhumanity of slavery, students can see how slavery benefited many White people economically and served their financial interests. Being aware of these perspectives can help students understand why slavery persisted in the United States for so many years.

Furthermore, when we pair texts together because they share similar historical settings or similar themes, students can learn that history is more than just a single narrative. While the history books that students encounter in school may be told from the dominant or majority group's interpretation of history, seeing different perspectives juxtaposed through the pairing of children's literature can help students understand that nothing should ever be taken at face value. There are always multiple sides to any story, and as critically literate readers, it is our responsibility to consider these various points of view. In Chapter 7, we demonstrate how teachers might utilize the pairing texts strategy to help students consider multiple perspectives.

ANNOTATED BIBLIOGRAPHY

Alonso, Harriet Hyman. *Martha and the Slave Catchers*. Zunon, Elizabeth. 2017. 256 pp. Triangle Square. 9781609808006
Martha is the daughter of Connecticut abolitionists. When her adopted brother is kidnapped by slave catchers who claim he is the son of a fugitive that her parents once harbored, Martha leaves home on a dangerous journey to rescue him.

Behar, Ruth. *Lucky Broken Girl*. 2017. 256 pp. Nancy Paulsen Books. 9780399546440
A car accident leaves Ruthie bedridden for months. Anger and bitterness threaten to consume her, but Ruthie learns to find joy in an unfortunate circumstance, and importantly, she learns how to forgive.

Bradbury, Jennifer. *River Runs Deep*. 2015. 336 pp. Atheneum Books for Young Readers. 9781442468245
Elias has always taken for granted that Blacks are enslaved and Whites are the masters. When Elias becomes ill with consumption, he is sent to live in Mammoth Cave in hope of recovery. Elias challenges his old way of thinking when he gets to know Stephen, Nick, and Mat, three resourceful and intelligent enslaved men who work in the cave and operate a safe haven for those seeking their freedom.

Bradley, Kimberly Brubaker. *The War I Finally Won*. 2017. 400 pp. Dial Books. 9780525429203
In this sequel to *The War That Saved My Life*, Ada's life changes once more when she, Jamie, and their guardian Susan must move in with her best friend Maggie and frosty Lady Thornton. Life becomes even more complicated when Ruth, a Jewish teen from Germany, moves into the home, and everyone (Ada included) is forced to challenge their assumptions and open their hearts.

Bradley, Kimberly Brubaker. *The War That Saved My Life*. 2015. 320 pp. Dial Books. 9780803740815
Ada has never left home. Her clubfoot makes walking difficult, but worse, her mother's shame has forced her to stay hidden away for her entire life. When Hitler's bombs rain on London, Ada sneaks out with her younger brother Jamie as they flee to the English countryside and start a new life.

Bundy, Tamara. *Walking with Miss Millie*. 2017. 240 pp. Nancy Paulsen Books. 9780399544569
Alice is upset about moving to the small town of Rainbow, Georgia, but she soon finds a friend in her elderly neighbor Miss Millie. Through Miss Millie's stories, Alice learns about the cruel ways that segregation and racism have touched the lives of the people in her new town both past and present.

Choldenko, Gennifer. *Al Capone Throws Me a Curve*. 2018. 240 pp. Wendy Lamb Books. 9781101938133
Moose Flanagan's father is a prison guard on Alcatraz Island during the Great Depression, and Moose must learn to make friends and navigate complicated relationships all while keeping a close eye on his older sister Natalie, who has special needs and is sometimes viewed with suspicion and misunderstanding by others. In this latest installment in the Tales from Alcatraz series, Moose is forced to make a daring and dangerous rescue when Natalie enters the prison walls.

Cline-Ransome, Lesa. *Finding Langston*. 2018. 112 pp. Holiday House. 9780823439607
After his mother dies and Langston and his father move to Chicago, life becomes difficult and painful. But one day when he is trying to hide from bullies, Langston discovers a library, a place unlike anywhere he has ever seen before, and soon learns to take comfort in the words of his namesake, Langston Hughes.

Curtis, Christopher Paul. *The Journey of Little Charlie*. 2018. 256 pp. Scholastic Press. 9780545156660
Charlie takes both a literal and figurative journey as he travels to the North with ornery Cap'n Buck, a slave catcher. As they track down the runaways, Charlie is forced to challenge his assumptions about slavery and the supposed inferiority of Black Americans.

Draper, Sharon M. *Stella by Starlight*. 2015. 336 pp. Atheneum Books for Young Readers. 9781442494972
Stella, her family, and their neighbors and friends must muster their strength and resilience when a series of events, including activity by the Ku Klux Klan, threaten their segregated Southern community during the Great Depression years.

Duncan, Alice Faye. *Memphis, Martin, and the Mountaintop: The Sanitation Strike of 1968*. Christie, R. Gregory. 2018. 40 pp. Calkins Creek. 9781629797182
Based on real people and actual events, this is a fictionalized account of the sanitation strike preceding Martin Luther King Jr.'s assassination told from the perspective of a young girl.

Elvgren, Jennifer. *The Edelweiss Pirates*. Stamatiadi, Daniela. 2018. 32 pp. Kar-Ben Publishing. 9781512483604
Kurt wants to be an Edelweiss Pirate likes his older brother Albert, who plays forbidden jazz music in defiance of Hitler's rules. As Kurt begins to notice the injustices that his Jewish friends and neighbors face, he uses his passion for music to take a stand.

Gratz, Alan. *Refugee*. 2017. 352 pp. Scholastic Press. 9780545880831
Alternating chapters tell the immigration stories of Josef, a Jewish boy in Nazi Germany; Isabel, a Cuban girl living under Castro's rule in the early 1990s; and Mahmoud, a contemporary Syrian boy. Their stories converge with a surprising twist at the end.

Hargrave, Kiran Millwood. *The Island at the End of Everything*. 2018. 256 pp. Knopf Books for Young Readers. 9780553535327
Culion, an island in the Philippines, is a haven for people with Hansen's disease (leprosy), and it is the only home Ami has known. When she and other unaffected children are forced to leave the island by a cruel government official, Ami embarks on a desperate journey back to see her ailing mother.

Klages, Ellen. *Out of Left Field*. 2018. 320 pp. Viking Books for Young Readers. 9780425288591
Disguised as a boy, talented pitcher Katy Gordon makes it onto a Little League team, but she is promptly kicked off when her true identity as a girl is discovered. It is 1957, and girls are not allowed to play organized baseball. Katy decides to fight back and embarks on a quest to prove that women have always had a place in baseball history.

Nolen, Jerdine. *Calico Girl*. 2017. 192 pp. Simon & Schuster/Paula Wiseman Books. 9781481459813
Callie and her family are enslaved, but they are given a new hope for their future when a community for Black families is established at Fort Monroe, a stronghold for the Union in Virginia.

Stamper, Vesper. *What the Night Sings*. 2018. 272 pp. Knopf Books for Young Readers. 9781524700386
> Gerta did not know she was Jewish until the day her family is betrayed and she is sent to a concentration camp. Gerta survives the atrocities of the Holocaust, and when the war ends, she carves out a new life for herself in Palestine with her new husband, Lev.

Weaver, Lila Quintero. *My Year in the Middle*. 2018. 288 pp. Candlewick. 9780763692315
> Lu is the daughter of Argentinian immigrants living in small-town Alabama in 1970. As her school becomes integrated, Lu is stuck in the middle between her White friends, who support segregationist George Wallace, and a new Black friend, Belinda, who shares her passion and talent for running.

Wolk, Lauren. *Beyond the Bright Sea*. 2017. 304 pp. Dutton Books for Young Readers. 9781101994856
> Crow has a happy life with her adopted father Osh and their friendly neighbor Miss Maggie, but she has always wondered why other people in their small island community avoid her. When Crow learns her birth family may have come from Pekinese, a neighboring island that was once a leper colony, she becomes determined to uncover the truth.

Wolk, Lauren. *Wolf Hollow*. 2016. 304 pp. Dutton Books for Young Readers. 9781101994825
> When tragedy strikes in Annabelle's rural community, suspicions are quickly cast on Toby, an eccentric, homeless man. Annabelle takes action to protect Toby from her neighbors' prejudice and works to uncover the truth.

7

Pairing Texts to Expand Perspectives
(Lesson Plan)

As we discussed in Chapter 6, the history and social studies textbooks that students encounter in school sometimes show only one perspective of an event or a period in time. Danielle (first author) recalls her high school social studies teacher comparing a U.S. history textbook to a "fish stick": bland and boring. As a result of their experiences with these texts, students may take away a narrow, one-sided, or even distorted view of history. Of course, we know that history is not neutral, and there is never one "single story" (Adichie, 2009). The critical literacy strategy of pairing texts can help students understand the complexities of historical events and know that history comprises multiple stories. When we pair texts about similar topics that offer different perspectives, students can see that what authors choose to highlight in textbooks and children's trade books is subjective. Authors make purposeful decisions about whose side of the story they want to tell based on their own beliefs, motivations, and interests. As discussed in Chapter 1, considering multiple perspectives is an element of critical literacy. Pairing texts is one way that teachers can achieve this goal using historical fiction.

In this chapter, we return to Robert's fifth-grade classroom. Robert teaches both English language arts and social studies, and he often develops interdisciplinary units that blend the two content areas. At this point in the school year, Robert's class is studying the years leading up to the American Civil War. Lately, he has been focusing his teaching on antebellum Americans' differing views of slavery, one of the major issues that would later ignite the Civil War. For this study, Robert asked his students to select one of two historical fiction novels to read: *Martha and the Slave Catchers* or *The Journey of Little Charlie*. The former tells the story of Martha, the daughter of Connecticut abolitionists, who journeys to Maryland to rescue her adopted brother Jake, the son of a runaway slave who is stolen by his birth mother's former master. In the latter text, Charlie belongs to a Southern sharecropping family, and he becomes obligated to travel to the North with a devious slave catcher to pay back a debt owed by his recently deceased father. Charlie takes a journey both literally and figuratively as he leaves the South for the first time and begins to recognize African Americans as human beings not so different from himself. Charlie's character demonstrates the true meaning of critical literacy when he begins to push back against and question the lies he has been told about Black people. Both stories are set in the years between the passing of the Fugitive Slave Act, which allowed slave owners to "reclaim" enslaved people who had run away to freedom in the Northern states, and the Civil War.

These texts make a meaningful pairing for the purpose of Robert's lesson. While they have the historical setting in common, they show students the different viewpoints that White people in particular had of slavery in the years leading up to the Civil War. While Martha is staunchly abolitionist and witnesses her parents assist enslaved people who have run away, Charlie is largely ignorant. He understands that Cap'n Buck, the slave catcher and overseer whom he accompanies to the North, is unduly cruel to the enslaved people at a nearby plantation. However, he sees slavery as a fact of life. He believes that traveling to the North with Cap'n Buck to capture two runaways is justifiable: "The righteous, Christian thing about going north with Cap'n Buck was that by bringing thieves back to pay for their sins, we's helping to right a great wrong" (p. 80). It is not until Charlie meets and gets to know a Black youth his own age that he begins to change his mind and question the horrors of slavery and the Fugitive Slave Act.

Over the last week, Robert's students have been reading and discussing their novel in small groups with other students who chose the same book. Now that everyone has finished reading their book, Robert wants the whole class to join together and compare and contrast the perspectives presented in the two novels. Ideally, Robert would have liked all of his students to read both *Martha and the Slave Catchers* and *The Journey of Little Charlie*, but with the limited amount of time he has to teach his demanding curriculum, he knew this was not possible. Instead, Robert decided to allow his students to choose which book to read and use a discussion strategy called *concentric circles* to expose students to the perspectives in both novels. According to Gonzalez (2015), in the concentric circles discussion strategy, students create two circles: one inside circle and one outside circle. Students on the inside face a partner on the outside. After being prompted by the teacher, the students spend several minutes discussing a topic together. When it is time for the next questions, students in the outer circle rotate so that students have a new discussion partner. Depending on the amount of time allotted and the amount of questions the teacher wants students to discuss, students will have the opportunity to talk with multiple partners. This strategy is sometimes also called "speed dating."

After Robert's students participate in their concentric circle discussion, they move into a whole class discussion to synthesize the big ideas they learned from reading and talking about both books. Table 7.1 describes how a lesson like this one could be implemented in a fifth-grade classroom.

Table 7.1 Lesson Plan

Central focus: Students will *analyze* the similarities and differences between characters' perspectives of slavery in two historical fiction novels.	Subject: English language arts and social studies
Grade: 5	Classroom context: Whole group

Standards

CCSS.ELA-LITERACY.RL.5.1: Quote accurately from a text when explaining what the text says explicitly and when drawing inferences from the text.

CCSS.ELA-LITERACY.RL.5.9: Compare and contrast stories in the same genre (e.g., mysteries and adventure stories) on their approaches to similar themes and topics.

CCSS.ELA-LITERACY.SL.5.1: Engage effectively in a range of collaborative discussions (one-on-one, in groups, and teacher-led) with diverse partners on grade 5 topics and texts, building on others' ideas and expressing their own clearly.

CCSS.ELA-LITERACY.SL.5.1a. Come to discussions prepared, having read or studied required material; explicitly draw on that preparation and other information known about the topic to explore ideas under discussion.

Objectives

Students will *know* the perspective of slavery held by different groups of antebellum-era Americans, including Northern abolitionists and Southern Whites.

Students will *understand* that life experiences and cultural group membership informs people's perspectives of ethical, moral, and social issues.

Students will *be able to* compare and contrast the different views of slavery expressed by characters in historical fiction novels and justify their analysis using evidence from the text.

Assessment: The teacher may assess students formatively in this lesson by listening to students' concentric circles discussions and their participation in the whole class discussion. When listening, the teacher should consider whether students are citing specific details or quotes from their assigned book, making relevant and meaningful contributions to the discussion and demonstrating positive behaviors such as making eye contact with peers and speaking audibly and clearly. Teachers may opt to use or modify a discussion rubric such as the one at http://studentvote.ca/oncivic2014/wp-content/uploads/2014/09/ELE-EN-Discussion-Skills-and-Participation-Rubric.pdf to assess the effectiveness of students' participation in the discussion.

In addition, the teacher can formatively assess students' "before" and "after" responses on the Padlet. As explained in Steps 2 and 11, students complete a quick write on the Padlet in response to the question: *Why did White people have different views about slavery in the years before the Civil War?* By reviewing students' responses on the Padlet, the teacher can see if the discussion assisted students with meeting the lesson objectives.

(Continued)

Table 7.1   Lesson Plan (Continued)

Materials

- Each student should have a copy of *Martha and the Slave Catchers* or *The Journey of Little Charlie*.
- The teacher should have a list of both concentric circle discussion questions and whole class discussion questions related to the lesson objectives. (Sample questions are included in the Work Session section.)
- The teacher should create a free Padlet at www.padlet.com. The Padlet should be set up in two columns: Introduction and Closure. Students will require a tablet or laptop to access the Padlet.
- Copies of the Discussion Graphic Organizer (see Figure 7.1 at the end of this lesson plan)

Academic language function: Analyze	**Language demands:** Reading a grade-level text, speaking with peers about a text, listening to peers speak about a text

Lesson introduction

1. The teacher sets the purpose of the lesson: "We have been studying about slavery in our social studies unit, especially about the attitudes and beliefs that White people had toward slavery. You have read either *Martha and the Slave Catchers* or *The Journey of Little Charlie*. Both books take place during the same time period: after the passing of the Fugitive Slave Act, which we have studied, and the Civil War, which we will study soon. During today's class, we are going to discuss the reasons *why* people held certain views of slavery, especially White people, who are the ones who had political power back then. Later when we study more about the Civil War, this discussion will help you understand why people went to war over slavery among other reasons. You will participate in two discussions today: a partner discussion activity and a whole class discussion."

2. The teacher introduces the Padlet quick writing activity to activate students' prior knowledge (and to use for assessment later). The teacher instructs students to take out their tablets, computers, or other Internet-enabled devices. "Please pull up the link to the Padlet that I have posted on our class website. On the Padlet, you will see two columns labeled 'Introduction' and 'Closure.' For now, you will write your answer in the 'Introduction' column. On the Padlet, please type your answer to this question: *Why did White people have different views about slavery in the years before the Civil War?* Remember to include your name on your Padlet post."

Instructional input

3. The teacher says, "Before we begin our discussion, you are going to prepare by brainstorming with other students who read the same book as you." The teacher hands out the Discussion Graphic Organizer. "Please talk about the questions on your graphic organizer with your group members and take notes. Make sure that you use evidence or reasons from your book to support your answers. You may refer to this graphic organizer during the discussion we will have soon." The teacher provides the students time to work in their groups and take notes on the graphic organizer.

4. The teacher explains, "Next, we are going to discuss the books *Martha and the Slave Catchers* and *The Journey of Little Charlie*. We will stand up for this discussion and form two circles, one inside and one outside. If you read *Martha*, you will stand inside. If you read *Charlie*, you will stand outside. Your partner will be the person in the opposite circle. You will face your partner. When I read a question, you and your partner will have several minutes to take turns discussing the question based on the book that you read. You will teach each other about how different groups of people felt about slavery before the Civil War. After the time is up, those of you in the outside circle will take a step to the right so you are facing a new partner. Then I will ask another question. We will do this several times. Are there any questions about this?" The teacher allows time to respond to students' questions.

Work session

5. The students organize into an inner circle and an outer circle based on the teacher's instructions in Step 4. Students may bring their completed graphic organizers from Step 3. Each student faces a partner. The teacher poses the first question: "How did the protagonist of your book feel about slavery and why?" Students spend several minutes discussing the question. The teacher may either set a timer or wait until conversation dies down before posing the next question in Step 6.

6. The teacher says, "Students in the outer circle, please take a step to your right and face your new partner." The teacher poses the next question: "How did your character's family feel about slavery and why?" Students are given time to discuss this question with their new partners.

7. The teacher repeats Step 6 several times. Other questions the teacher may ask include:

   - *What experiences did your character have with enslaved people or slavery?*
   - *Did your character's feelings about slavery change, and how?*
   - *What did your character do to act out against slavery, if anything? What motivated your character to do this?*
   - *Both Charlie and Martha met slave catchers in the books. How did their views of slavery differ from those of the slave catchers?*
   - *If your character was Black instead of White, how do you think his, her, or their feelings about slavery would be the same or different?*

8. After wrapping up the concentric circle discussion activity, the teacher asks students to sit on the carpet for a whole class discussion. The teacher says, "Now you have learned some different views of slavery from hearing about each other's books. We are going to have a discussion as a whole group so we can put together, or synthesize, the different views that we have learned about from our books." The questions that will be asked in the remaining steps of the lesson are broader in scope and are designed to help students arrive at the main idea stated in the "understand" objective of this lesson plan.

(Continued)

Table 7.1 Lesson Plan (Continued)

9. The teacher introduces the first question of the whole class discussion: *What perspectives did White people have toward enslaved people prior to the Civil War?* The students raise their hands and are called on to share; they are encouraged to elaborate on each other's ideas and ask each other questions. They are also asked to think about all of the characters they encountered in the books, not just protagonists Martha and Charlie. The teacher should listen for whether students are using evidence from their books in their responses.

10. When the class is ready to move on, the teacher poses the next question. Other questions relating to the discussion purpose might include:

- *Based on the novels and what we have studied in our class, what generalizations can you make about what people believed about slavery? Did certain groups of people tend to have similar beliefs?*

- *How were people's beliefs about slavery shaped? Can you make generalizations?*

- *What effect did these perspectives of slavery have on people's actions and behavior?*

- *Could there be other beliefs about slavery that we did not learn from reading these books? Whose voices are missing from these books? What might these voices have to say?*

- *What did you learn about slavery from reading these books that you haven't learned in our class or other classes?*

Lesson closure

11. After the discussion is over, the teacher shares the link to the Padlet once again and asks students to take out their Internet-enabled devices. The teacher says, "Reflect on what you read in your novel and all that we have talked about in our class today. I'd like you to answer the same question that you responded to earlier—*Why did White people have different views about slavery in the years before the Civil War?*—on the Padlet. Later, I will compare what you wrote in the introduction and what you write now to help me understand what you learned."

Differentiation

The lesson is differentiated by interest and readiness because students have the choice of reading either *Martha and the Slave Catchers* or *The Journey of Little Charlie*, which is a more complex text. Students who need assistance with reading could be given audio books or e-books with text-to-speech functionality.

Students who require support with contributing to the discussion may refer to the graphic organizer completed with peers in Step 3 in both the concentric circle and whole class discussions.

Students who would benefit from a challenge and have proficient reading skills could be asked to read excerpts from primary source texts like *Narrative of the Life of Frederick Douglass* or *Incidents in the Life of a Slave Girl* by Harriet Jacobs for homework prior to the discussion. These students could integrate these additional perspectives into the discussions for the purpose of comparing and contrasting the views of people who actually experienced slavery with the views of the fictionalized characters in the two novels.

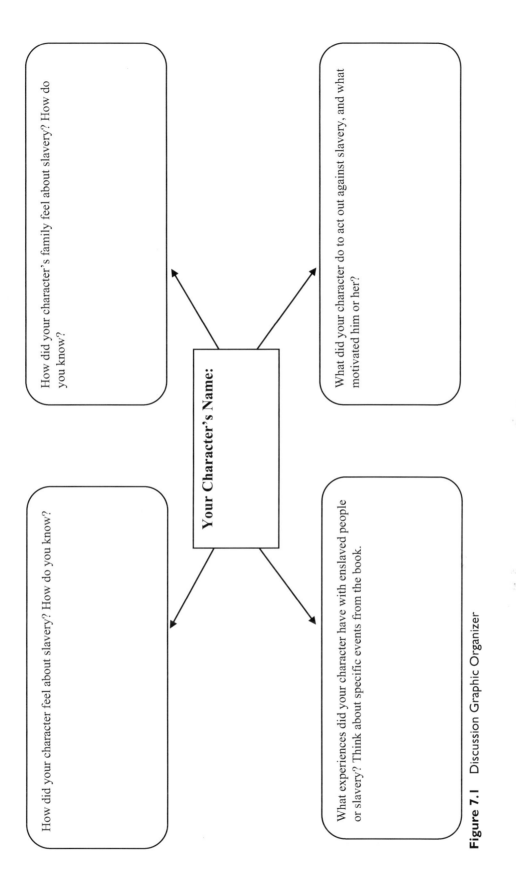

Figure 7.1 Discussion Graphic Organizer

The four surrounding boxes contain:

- How did your character's family feel about slavery? How do you know?

- What did your character do to act out against slavery, and what motivated him or her?

- How did your character feel about slavery? How do you know?

- What experiences did your character have with enslaved people or slavery? Think about specific events from the book.

Center box: **Your Character's Name:**

MODIFYING THE LESSON PLAN

Obviously, the concentric circles discussion strategy would be most effective if an equal number of students read the two novels (e.g., ten students read *Martha and the Slave Catchers* and ten students read *The Journey of Little Charlie*). This way, an individual student would always be conversing with a peer who read a different novel. However, if the numbers of students who read each novel are not approximately equal, teachers could select an alternative discussion strategy for Steps 5–7. For example, two or three students who read each book could be placed in a small group and asked to discuss the questions together.

The approaches to class discussions that we have explained in this chapter may be implemented in any of the grade levels targeted in this book. The critical literacy strategy of pairing texts to expand perspectives of a topic may also be used in any grade from four through eight. Of course, the choice of texts will vary depending on the teacher's curriculum and the readiness of students. The school librarian is an excellent resource to consult to identify appropriate pairs of books. The following are several other pairing possibilities:

- Students could explore a historical perspective of how people with disabilities have been treated by reading *The War That Saved My Life* and *Al Capone Throws Me a Curve*. Both novels feature major characters with a disability: Ada in *The War That Saved My Life* has a clubfoot, and Natalie in *Al Capone Throws Me a Curve* has autism. Examining these two books could prompt students to wonder if people with disabilities experience better treatment today and what social, cultural, and political changes led to this change.

- Students can interrogate the question "Why do some people become outcasts by society?" by reading a pair of Lauren Wolk's books, *Beyond the Bright Sea* and *Wolf Hollow*. In *Beyond the Bright Sea*, Crow discovers that people keep their distance from her because they suspect her parents were lepers, while in *Wolf Hollow*, Toby is shunned by many people in his small community because of his homelessness and perceived strangeness. Through interrogating this question, students may realize that people often fear what is different or strange. This may lead to students generating other, more contemporary examples of groups or individuals who are considered "outcasts" and taking actions to promote more inclusive classrooms, schools, neighborhoods, and communities.

- To examine how Jewish people were treated in the early- and mid-twentieth century, upper elementary students could read *The War I Finally Won* and *The Edelweiss Pirates*, while older children could read *Refugee* and *What the Night Sings*. Reading the perspectives in these books could prompt students to wonder "Why have Jewish people been history's scapegoats?" and "Who are the scapegoats of today's society and why? Whose interests are served when scapegoating a group of people?"

8

Contemporary Realistic Fiction

Hannah's seventh-grade English class has been studying the genre of contemporary realistic fiction. Small groups of Hannah's students are scattered around the classroom; each group is reading and discussing a different title from this genre. One group is reading Breakout *by Kate Messner, a novel about a prison escape in a rural upstate New York community told from the perspective of three seventh-grade girls: Nora and Lizzie, who are White and have always lived in Wolf Creek, and Elidee, who is Black and moved to Wolf Creek recently to be close to her brother, an inmate at the prison. Before they gathered in their small groups, Hannah taught her students a mini-lesson about making disconnections, a strategy that can be used for promoting reading comprehension and helping students develop a critical literacy stance (Jones & Clarke, 2007).*

As Hannah walks over to the Breakout *group and listens to their discussion, she can tell the students are using the strategy to unpack the significant social issues explored in the book. "I have a disconnection," Luke declares. "On page 175, Elidee writes that her mom taught her to act calm if she's ever confronted by the police. This is a disconnection because my mom never talked to me about how to act around the police. She always told me to run to an officer if I thought I was in trouble. Elidee was probably taught that the police are scary, but I was taught they are there to keep me safe." Michelle, a fellow group member, uses Luke's disconnection as an invitation to dig deeper, just as Hannah taught the students in her mini-lesson. "Why do we think Elidee's mother would need to tell Elidee how to act in front of the police? And why would Luke's mother would tell him to go find the police if something is wrong?" she asks her group. The students in the group begin sharing ideas, and eventually, the conversation turns to recent events in the news media about racial bias in the police force; students recall several occasions where violent acts were committed against Black individuals by the police. Students realize that bias against Black people could lead Elidee, a Black character, and Luke, a White student, to have differing perspectives of the police. As the group continues to talk about this topic, Hannah is pleased that her students have used the making disconnections strategy to notice and name real social inequities. Hannah knows that contemporary realistic fiction books like* Breakout *can help her students understand social justice issues and take a critical view of their world. In Chapter 9, we will take a closer look at how teachers can apply the making disconnections strategy to support critical literacy.*

DEFINING CONTEMPORARY REALISTIC FICTION

The genre of contemporary realistic fiction is sometimes called "contemporary realism" or "realistic fiction." Regardless of the term used, books belonging to this genre are works of fiction set in the present day or in the very recent past. For example, a book set in 2015 such as Joanne Rocklin's *Love, Penelope* belongs to the contemporary realistic fiction genre. As mentioned in Chapter 6, we are defining contemporary realistic fiction as books set in the year 2000 or later. Of course, this chronological marker must shift as time advances. The year 2000 will one day seem like the distant past even to adults.

Sometimes contemporary realistic fiction books feature actual events in recent history as a backdrop to the story. In *Love, Penelope*, the title character's two moms decide to get married after the Supreme Court's historic decision recognizing the legality of same-sex marriages. In *Towers Falling* by Jewell Parker Rhodes, fifth grader Déja learns how the tragic events of September 11, 2001, are linked to her father's sadness and depression years later. Noticing actual events appearing in fictional children's books can help educators determine whether a book should be considered contemporary or historical.

It is important to mention that books with seemingly timeless stories and settings may also be considered contemporary realistic fiction. While we are focusing on recently published books for the purpose of this text (titles published in 2014 or later), older books such as Judy Blume's *Tales of a Fourth Grade Nothing* (published in 1972) and Katherine Paterson's *Bridge to Terabithia* (published in 1977) would also be considered contemporary realistic fiction. Though they were published more than forty years ago, these stories include themes and characters that continue to appeal to contemporary children. In addition, they are set in a nonspecific time period. These stories could easily take place today.

Although the events occurring in contemporary realistic fiction books are imagined by their authors, they must be realistic, meaning they could actually happen in real life. There are no magical or supernatural elements in realistic fiction. However, sometimes the events in a realistic fiction book can seem highly improbable. In Amy Sarig King's *Me and Marvin Gardens*, sixth-grader Obe discovers a previously unknown species of animal that eats plastic and consequently produces environmentally toxic scat. Obe names the animal "Marvin Gardens," and he must convince adults that his discovery is real and persuade them to protect Marvin Gardens and his offspring. Is it likely that a sixth grader would discover an entirely new species that prefers eating plastic? No. Is it possible? Yes. New species are discovered often (though not usually by sixth graders), and as we have learned the hard way as pet owners, even some dogs and cats will eat plastic items if given the opportunity. As improbable as some events in *Me and Marvin Gardens* might seem, they could still happen in real life, and the book is thus considered an example of contemporary realistic fiction. Unlike works of fantasy, which include events that are impossible, contemporary realistic fiction books include events that *could* possibly happen in the real world even if they are not likely to happen.

We read contemporary realistic fiction to better understand the world through the perspectives of others. Importantly, realistic fiction books feature characters with problems that children can understand. In *Ghost* by Jason Reynolds, the title character runs track to cope with an unthinkable event from his past: his father is in jail for shooting at Ghost and his mother. Sadly, some children reading this book may have experienced similar situations. However, even children who have not experienced domestic violence can relate to other feelings that Ghost experiences, such as a desire to fit in that compels Ghost to shoplift a pair of silver sneakers from an athletic store. Many children can understand the need to own the "right" clothing or the "right" pair of shoes to fit in at school or with a peer group.

Contemporary realistic fiction books offer students the chance to learn about and empathize with situations that they or their peers may have actually experienced. For example, *Forever, or a Long, Long Time* by Caela Carter and *Hope in the Holler* by Lisa Lewis Tyre can help children understand the loss of family and the challenges experienced by children placed in the foster care system. *Rain Reign* by Ann M. Martin, *Fish in a Tree* by Lynda Mullaly Hunt, and *As Brave As You* by Jason Reynolds provide insight into the lives and problems faced by people with cognitive or physical disabilities. Most children in today's public schools are likely to encounter a peer in the foster care system or a peer who is differently abled, or they may be in foster care or diagnosed with a cognitive or physical disability themselves. Although books in this genre are fictional, they give children the opportunity to learn about the realities of the world through realistic characters facing situations that children can recognize even if they have not personally experienced them. Themes in contemporary realistic fiction are relevant to children's lives.

The contemporary realistic fiction books published today for middle-grade readers often feature social issues that mirror those we see in the present time. For example, brutality against Black people by some members of the police force is a serious social problem in our time. Books like *The Hate U Give* by Angie Thomas, *Piecing Me Together* by Renée Watson, *All American Boys* by Jason Reynolds and Brendan Kiely, and *Anger Is a Gift* by Mark Oshiro include these issues, and although the events in them are made up by their authors, they could easily be ripped from today's headlines. Other social issues are also evident in contemporary realistic fiction books:

- Acceptance of lesbian, gay, bisexual, queer/questioning, and transgender people is addressed in *George* by Alex Gino. The title character was born a male but identifies as female, and she must convince others to accept her true self.

- Hate crimes and anti-Muslim bias are tackled in *Amina's Voice* by Hena Khan when the mosque Amina and her family attend is vandalized.

- Nora and her friends discover the effects of racial bias in the criminal justice system in *Breakout*.
- Bullying is evident in *Fish in a Tree*. Sixth-grader Ally is dyslexic and doesn't know how to read, resulting in teasing by her classmates.
- Homelessness is confronted in *Towers Falling* as Déja and her family reside in a homeless shelter and try to make ends meet.
- Zoey deals with poverty and the unraveling of her family due to domestic abuse in *The Benefits of Being an Octopus* by Ann Braden.

Although the inclusion of social issues is not a requirement for a book to be classified as contemporary realistic fiction, many books published for youth today promote awareness of social injustice and inequality, making these books excellent launching points for critical discussions as we saw in this chapter's opening vignette.

EVALUATING REALISTIC FICTION

There are several criteria to consider when evaluating books in the contemporary realistic fiction genre. First, educators must decide whether the book is truly realistic. If a book features events that could happen in reality (even if they are improbable), then the book is realistic. If a book includes events that could never happen in present-day real life, then it should not be considered part of the contemporary realistic fiction genre. The settings and events in contemporary realistic fiction books must seem believable although they are imagined. In other words, situations in contemporary realistic fiction books *could* be true even though they are not.

Authors often develop realism through vivid descriptions of the characters and settings. In *Hope in the Holler*, the death of Wavie's mother forces Wavie into the foster care system, and she is sent to live with Samantha Rose, an aunt she has never met. Author Lisa Lewis Tyre's detailed description of Samantha Rose's house helps capture Wavie's dismay toward her new home:

> I stared out the window. The first thing I noticed was the trash. Soda bottles, scraps of paper, and waterlogged books littered the yard. A recliner with the stuffing coming out of it sat in a tangle of weeds next to some old cars and a rusty barrel. . . . The house itself looked old as the devil and about as inviting. The front porch was crooked and crammed full of junk, too. I couldn't imagine living in that place. (p. 19)

Rich descriptions like this one can also provide readers with a sense of place as they read realistic fiction; in *Hope in the Holler*, readers are drawn into Wavie's world of impoverished, rural Appalachia. Educators should look for these kinds of descriptions when selecting books for classroom use or school libraries.

It is especially important for the characters in contemporary realistic fiction to be realistic. Their actions, personalities, and speech should resemble those of real people. The character of Lolly in *The Stars beneath Our Feet* by David Barclay

Moore is a great example of this. Lolly is in middle school, and he copes with the loss of his older brother, Jermaine, by building fantastical creations with Legos. Lolly is far from perfect. Just like a real young person, he has feelings that range from sadness to anger to fear to awe. He can be a kind person, but he makes mistakes and sometimes passes unfair judgments on his peers. Lolly speaks in African American Vernacular, the language often spoken in his native Harlem: " 'Aw, God! Why you bringing him up? He's okay,' [Lolly] said" (p. 59). In fact, Moore writes in his author's note, "One of the reasons that I wanted to write *The Stars beneath Our Feet* is that there aren't enough books that speak with the voices of the characters in my story." Presumably, Moore authored this book so that young people sharing cultural identities similar to Lolly's could see themselves represented in children's literature. Indeed, high-quality realistic fiction should give children a chance to meet characters with lives similar to their own or with lives similar to people they might encounter in real life either now or in the future. Realistic fiction falls short when characters do not seem real and relatable to young people.

Additionally, educators should evaluate contemporary realistic fiction by considering whether a book can help children cope with their own problems. In *The Epic Fail of Arturo Zamora* by Pablo Cartaya, Arturo faces the loss of his beloved Abeula and the gentrification of his beloved, family-oriented community by a greedy developer. Arturo becomes inspired by the work of Cuban poet José Martí and begins writing his own poetry to process his grief and fear. Similarly, Nora in *Breakout* writes letters for a time capsule project to express her worries about the escaped convicts roaming around her community. (We suspect English teachers will be particularly charmed by Arturo's and Nora's coping strategy.) Other characters in realistic fiction use different strategies to cope with the situations they face. Jade in *Piecing Me Together* creates collages to bolster her confidence and process her feelings, Ben and Charlotte in *You Go First* compete in an online Scrabble game to handle their loneliness, and Lolly and his friend Rose in *The Stars beneath Our Feet* turn to building with Legos to deal with the loss of beloved family members. All of these are healthy and feasible outlets that children can emulate if they face similar problems in their own lives. Though contemporary realistic fiction books offer life lessons to children, educators should be mindful that books with overly didactic tones can be unappealing to young people. The lessons learned from reading realistic fiction should arise naturally from the story line.

Good realistic fiction should also help children feel empathy toward people whose lives are different from their own. In *Fish in a Tree*, Ally is the friendless troublemaker in her sixth-grade class who often acts out or does things to garner the disapproval of her peers and teachers. In the beginning of the book, Ally gives her pregnant teacher a sympathy card at the class baby shower. Ally's classmates are disgusted with her, but she feels terrible: "I feel real bad. . . . I just didn't know it was a sad card like that. All I could see were beautiful yellow flowers" (p. 10). As readers who are aware of Ally's struggles with reading, we can empathize with her and understand her mistake of giving a sympathy card to a pregnant woman. Many children can likely think of a classmate who reminds them of Ally. Although reading a book like *Fish in a Tree* can never truly help students understand the daily challenges faced by people with dyslexia like Ally, books like these can help children be more understanding and sensitive to classmates who face similar struggles. And for students who do face a situation like Ally's, books like *Fish in a Tree* can help them feel less alone. In a society that is becoming increasingly pluralistic, it is critical for educators to select contemporary realistic fiction that can help readers grow respect and empathy for others.

In addition to these criteria, special considerations should be given to evaluating multicultural contemporary realistic fiction books. If educators are selecting realistic fiction books with diverse characters, they should preferably choose books authored by cultural insiders who are writing from positions of respect and deep knowledge about the culture represented. Such books are often described in social media with the label #OwnVoices, which means "diverse books written by diverse creators" (Gómez, 2017, para. 3). For example, *Amina's Voice* is about a Pakistani American family who worship at a mosque in Milwaukee. As the book's jacket flap indicates, author Hena Khan is a member of this cultural group. Likewise, Pablo Cartaya writes about the world he knows by setting *The Epic Fail of Arturo Zamora* in his home city of Miami, and Lynda Mullaly Hunt's own experiences of struggling in school gave her insight into the character of Ally, the protagonist of *Fish in a Tree*. Sometimes authors create characters with cultural identities that differ from their own. In such cases, authors should thoughtfully research the culture they are representing and, preferably, ask a cultural insider or person with experiences similar to those depicted in the book to vet the manuscript for respect and accuracy. Educators who are unsure if a book accurately depicts a cultural group may want to consider reading blogs written by cultural insiders and experts. Table 8.1 lists blogs that currently review or raise awareness of multicultural books from a range of genres. In addition, educators seeking high-quality multicultural literature from any genre should consider selecting award-winning books that have been reviewed by children's literature experts. Table 8.2 provides a list of multicultural awards to help educators get started. The nonprofit organization We Need Diverse Books also provides an excellent list of resources for locating multicultural books on its website, https://diversebooks.org.

Table 8.1   Blogs Reviewing Multicultural Children's Literature

Blog Name	URL
American Indians in Children's Literature	https://americanindiansinchildrensliterature.blogspot.com/
The Brown Bookshelf	https://thebrownbookshelf.com/
Disability in Kid Lit	http://disabilityinkidlit.com/
Hijabi Librarians	https://hijabilibrarians.wordpress.com/
Latinx in Kid Lit	https://latinosinkidlit.com/

Table 8.2 Multicultural Book Awards

Award	Purpose	URL
Arab American Book Awards	Recognize books written by and about Arab Americans	http://www.arabamerican museum.org/bookaward
Asian/Pacific American Award for Literature	Recognizes books written about Asian/Pacific Americans	http://www.apalaweb.org/ awards/literature-awards/
Coretta Scott King Book Awards	Recognize books written by African Americans that celebrate African American culture	http://www.ala.org/rt/ emiert/cskbookawards
Mildred L. Batchelder Award	Recognizes international, translated books	http://www.ala.org/alsc/ awardsgrants/bookmedia/ batchelderaward
Notable Books for a Global Society	Recognizes books that help children develop global understanding	https://www.clrsig.org/ notable-books-for-a-global- society-nbgs.html
Pura Belpré Award	Recognizes books written by Latinx writers that celebrate Latinx culture	http://www.ala.org/alsc/ awardsgrants/bookmedia/ belpremedal
Schneider Family Book Award	Recognizes books that portray the experience of having a disability	http://www.ala.org/ awardsgrants/schneider- family-book-award
Stonewall Book Awards	Recognize books portraying the experiences of lesbian, gay, bisexual, and transgender people	http://www.ala.org/rt/glbtrt/ award/stonewall
United States Board on Books for Young People Outstanding International Books List	Recognizes books that portray international and global perspectives	https://www.usbby.org/ outstanding-international- books-list.html

READING CONTEMPORARY REALISTIC FICTION WITH A CRITICAL LITERACY LENS

We read contemporary realistic fiction to learn about ourselves and others and to understand the realities of our world. Because of the realism and relatability of this genre, one strategy that works particularly well for introducing students to critical literacy is making *dis*connections (Jones & Clarke, 2007). Many educators are likely familiar with the comprehension strategy of making connections. Readers are invited to consider links between a text and their own lives (text to self); other texts including magazines, films, television shows, and music (text to text); and actual local, national, or global events (text to world). Table 8.3 provides an example of how one reader might make connections to Kate Messner's *Breakout*.

Table 8.3   **Making Connections to *Breakout***

Type of Connection	Connection to *Breakout*
Text to self	Like Nora, I grew up in a small town in the Northeast, and the neighboring town was home to a state prison. People often moved to my hometown to be close to relatives in the prison much like Elidee and her mom.
Text to text	Nora slowly realizes that Blacks and Whites are still treated unequally in the United States, and she begins learning about White privilege. This makes me think of Quinn from the young adult novel *All American Boys* by Jason Reynolds and Brendan Kiely. After witnessing a police officer beat his Black classmate, Rashad, Quinn gradually awakens to the reality of racial inequality.
Text to world	The events in this book remind me of an event that happened last summer. Two inmates escaped from a prison in Georgia, where I live, and the search for them was broadcast all over the local and national news much like in *Breakout*.

As Jones and Clarke note, the making connections strategy has a theoretical basis in schema theory, and it is intended to help readers make sense of the text by activating their prior knowledge and linking what they already know to what they are presently reading. However, they explain that the making connections strategy encourages students to see similarities between their lives and the text. Consequently, students may assume the ideological stance of the text's author. Obviously, this is counter to critical literacy's goal of encouraging students to question and challenge the reality portrayed in the text. Moreover, Jones and Clarke argue that making connections is problematic because students will sometimes lay claim to realities that do not match their own lives and experiences. Students from the dominant culture might "co-opt" the experiences of marginalized groups when reading multicultural literature, and students from minority cultures will try to shape their experiences to match those of the dominant culture for the sake of making a connection and satisfying the teacher.

Jones and Clarke (2007) contend that educators should teach students how to make disconnections and maintain that making disconnections is a starting point for engaging in critical literacy. When students make disconnections with a text, they challenge the way the world is portrayed in the text and consider other realities. Disconnections urge readers to see how life is different for different people and invite them to examine the reasons why. To illustrate this idea, Table 8.4 shows disconnections that Danielle made to *Breakout* and how these disconnections could lead to additional questions that promote critically literate thinking.

Having conversations about questions like the ones shown in Table 8.4 can help students explore the different realities that people face because of their social and cultural identities. They help students consider new perspectives and illuminate

Table 8.4 Making Disconnections to *Breakout*

Disconnection	New Questions
Elidee's mom has difficulty finding a job in the small, predominantly White community of Wolf Creek, and Elidee's aunt is "pretty sure it's because people here aren't used to seeing names like Latanya on job applications" (p. 85). I cannot relate to Elidee's mom in this situation because I have never faced discrimination or lost opportunities because of assumptions people made about me for my name.	Was the name of Elidee's mom the reason why she wasn't hired for a job in Wolf Creek? What assumptions do people make when they hear names like "Latanya"? How do the assumptions that people make about names hurt others? How often are people who have uncommon names or names associated with a particular culture passed over when applying for jobs or college? Is bias against certain names a common occurrence? Are "White"-sounding names more accepted in American culture than names associated with other groups?
Elidee explains to Nora that "different people have to follow different rules in a place like [Wolf Creek]. Mama's always on me to watch my step, watch my mouth" (p. 273). This is a disconnection for me because as a White person, I don't have to be careful about what I say and do because in most situations, I am around people who look like me.	Do people in Wolf Creek scrutinize and judge Elidees's behavior more carefully because she is Black? Why do different people have different rules like Elidee claims, and who makes up these rules? Can a Black person like Elidee ever feel comfortable and welcomed in a predominantly White community and vice versa? Why does Elidee know about the "rules" for different people and Nora is ignorant?

Sidebar 8.1   Question Stems for Contemporary Realistic Fiction

- What social issues are addressed in the book, and how are they similar to social issues in the real world?
- What does the author think about the social issues addressed in the book? Why might the author have chosen to highlight these social issues?
- Are the themes and social issues in this book similar to other books from this genre? Why are these themes and issues so prevalent?
- What readers would recognize their own lives in this book? What readers might have difficulty with relating to this book and why?

---

the social inequities present in our society today. Asking and contemplating these questions is a main goal of critical literacy. In Chapter 9, we demonstrate how teachers can implement the strategy of making disconnections in the context of small-group, text-focused discussions.

ANNOTATED BIBLIOGRAPHY

Braden, Ann. *The Benefits of Being an Octopus*. 2018. 256 pp. Sky Pony Press. 9781510737488
Zoey wishes she could be more like an octopus. She would like nothing more than the ability to hide: to hide her poverty from her wealthy classmates, to hide her difficult homelife from her teachers, to hide her presence from her mother's unpredictable boyfriend. After a teacher forces her to join the debate team, Zoey realizes that hiding may not be the best solution to her problems after all.

Cartaya, Pablo. *The Epic Fail of Arturo Zamora*. 2017. 256 pp. Viking Books for Young Readers. 9781101997239
When Arturo loses his beloved abeula and a greedy developer sets his sights on gentrifying Arturo's neighborhood, Arturo takes inspiration in the work of Cuban poet José Martí and begins writing his own poetry to make sense of his grief and fear.

Carter, Caela. *Forever, or a Long, Long Time*. 2017. 320 pp. HarperCollins. 9780062385680
Flora and her brother Julian have been in so many foster homes that they can't remember where they came from or who their birth family was. When her adoptive mother becomes pregnant and Flora begins questioning her place in the family, she becomes compelled to uncover the secrets to her past.

Del Rizzo, Suzanne. *My Beautiful Birds*. 2017. 32 pp. Pajama Press. 9781772780109
When Sami's family is forced to flee their home and seek shelter in a refugee camp, Sami is devastated about leaving his feathery friends behind and wonders if his broken heart will ever heal.

Gino, Alex. *George*. 2015. 208 pp. Scholastic Press. 9780545812542
George was born a boy, but on the inside, he knows that he is a girl. With the help of Kelly, his best friend, George hatches a plan to show everyone his true self.

Hunt, Lynda Mullaly. *Fish in a Tree*. 2015. 288 pp. Nancy Paulsen Books. 9780399162596
Ally has been keeping a secret for a long time: she doesn't know how to read, and she masks her struggles by acting out and creating disruptions. But when a new teacher and new friends enter her life, Ally's troubles in school begin to turn around.

Kelly, Erin Entrada. *You Go First*. 2018. 304 pp. Greenwillow Books. 9780062414186
Ben and Charlotte have never met, but they stay connected through an online Scrabble game. Both experience the trials of middle school and learn the value of friendship to get through difficult times, especially when Ben is targeted by bullies.

Khan, Hena. *Amina's Voice*. 2017. 208 pp. Salaam Reads/Simon & Schuster Books for Young Readers. 9781481492065
Learning how to fit in and navigate friendships is hard enough for Amina. Life becomes even more challenging when her family's mosque is vandalized and Amina must confront anti-Muslim discrimination and hate.

King, Amy Sarig. *Me and Marvin Gardens*. 2017. 256 pp. Arthur A. Levine Books. 9780545870740
Lonely Obe befriends a strange animal and names him Marvin Gardens. After learning that Marvin Gardens might belong to a previously unknown species, Obe must figure out a way to share his discovery with scientists while taking measures to protect Marvin Gardens and his family.

Martin, Ann M. *Rain Reign*. 2014. 240 pp. Feiwel and Friends. 9780312643003
Getting a pet dog, Rain, is a wonderful event for Rose, an autistic girl who is friendless and often misunderstood. When Rain becomes lost in a storm and Rose learns that Rain once belonged to another family and was never truly hers to keep, she must make a difficult choice.

Messner, Kate. *Breakout*. 2018. 448 pp. Bloomsbury Children's Books. 9781681195360
This epistolary novel tells about the impact of a prison break on a small community. The breakout prompts Nora, the protagonist, to notice and question the racial
inequalities of the prison system.

Moore, David Barclay. *The Stars beneath Our Feet*. 2017. 304 pp. Knopf Books for Young
Readers. 9781524701246
Lolly is still coping with the loss of his older brother, who died in a gang-related
shooting. A gift of Legos and the formation of an unlikely friendship help Lolly
begin to heal.

Oshiro, Mark. *Anger Is a Gift*. 2018. 464 pp. Tor Teen. 9781250167026
Moss's urban high school feels more like a prison every day. A friend is brutalized by a school resource officer and metal detectors are installed, supposedly
to protect students. Fueled by these injustices and indignities, Moss and his
friends organize a walkout to call attention to the deep-seated problems at
their school.

Reynolds, Jason. *As Brave As You*. 2016. 432 pp. Atheneum/Caitlyn Dlouhy Books.
9781481415903
Genie is in for a memorable summer when his parents drop him and his cooler
older brother, Ernie, off at their grandparents' house while they sort through their
relationship troubles. At first, Genie is impressed by his blind grandfather's ability
to do everyday tasks without help. Yet several events prompt Genie to question
whether grandpop and Ernie are as brave as they seem.

Reynolds, Jason. *Ghost*. 2016. 192 pp. Atheneum/Caitlyn Dlouhy Books. 9781481450157
Running on a track team is good for Ghost; he makes new friends and finds a mentor in his coach. No matter how fast he is, Ghost wonders if he can ever outrun a
tragic event from his past.

Reynolds, Jason, & Kiely, Brendan. *All American Boys*. 2015. 320 pp. Atheneum/Caitlyn
Dlouhy Books. 9781481463331
Rashad, a Black teen, is brutalized by a police officer after being falsely accused
of stealing a bag of chips at a convenience store. Quinn, a White teen who attends
Rashad's school, witnesses the event. Told in alternating perspectives by Rashad
and Quinn, this novel calls attention to social problems such as police brutality,
racial discrimination, and the inequities of White privilege.

Rhodes, Jewell Parker. *Towers Falling*. 2016. 240 pp. Little, Brown Books for Young
Readers. 9780316262224
Déja lives in New York, but she has little knowledge of the events of September 11,
2001. When she starts at a new school in close proximity to Ground Zero, she
begins learning more about 9/11 and discovers her own family's connection to the
tragic events of that day.

Rocklin, Joanne. *Love, Penelope*. Lucy Knisely. 2018. 240 pp. Harry N. Abrams.
9781419728617
It's 2015. Penelope is looking forward to the birth of a new sibling, and her
favorite team, the Golden State Warriors, is heading toward a championship.
Though Penelope has many reasons to feel excited, she must grapple with
friendship problems, an unrequited crush, and antigay discrimination against
her two moms.

Thomas, Angie. *The Hate U Give*. 2017. 464 pp. Balzer + Bray. 9780062498533
Starr straddles two worlds: the mostly White private school she attends and the
working-class Black community she calls home. Though Starr tries to keep these
worlds separate, when she witnesses her childhood friend beaten to death by a
police officer, she is thrust in the middle of turmoil and must decide whether to
keep her head down or take a stand.

Tyre, Lisa Lewis. *Hope in the Holler.* 2018. 224 pp. Nancy Paulsen Books. 9780399546310

When her mother passes away, Wavie is thrust into the foster care system only to be "rescued" by her estranged Aunt Samantha Rose. It soon becomes clear to Wavie that her aunt has stepped forward only to collect a paycheck, and Wavie wonders if she will ever be able to escape her dire circumstances. However, the new friendships she makes in her small, rural community help Wavie cope and give her hope for a better future.

Watson, Renée. *Piecing Me Together.* 2017. 272 pp. Bloomsbury USA Childrens. 9781681191058

When Jade is offered an opportunity to participate in the Woman to Woman mentorship program, she is not interested. A Black teen from a "bad" urban neighborhood, Jade is tired of everyone's pity. The promise of a college scholarship is too much to pass up, though, and Jade reluctantly joins the program. However, she soon has to navigate a new set of problems as she copes with her unreliable and immature mentor, Maxine, and a tragedy in her community.

Making Disconnections in Literature Circles (Lesson Plan)

Chapter 8 described the strategy of making disconnections to contemporary realistic fiction books. When students make disconnections to what they read in a text, they notice how people and their experiences are different and are invited to wonder why. These new questions arising from making disconnections are entry points into critical literacy. Furthermore, the making disconnections strategy invites readers to "talk back" or resist the way people and events are portrayed in the text, which is an element of critical literacy addressed in Chapter 1.

Making disconnections to a text is highly personal. Readers can feel vulnerable when they are invited to disconnect their own lives, cultures, and experiences to those portrayed in a book and share these disconnections with peers. Moreover, when readers make disconnections to contemporary realistic fiction books that address significant social issues, students may find themselves discussing sensitive topics such as race and poverty. For these reasons, literature circles, which are small-group, student-led discussions about texts (Daniels, 2002), may offer a more comfortable setting for making and sharing disconnections. Students may be more open to exchanging ideas with a small peer group instead of with a whole class.

In addition to being a supportive setting for enacting critical literacy practices, literature circles benefit students in several other ways. Because students self-select their own books and lead their own discussions, literature circles are inherently differentiated according to students' readiness and interest (Daniels, 2002). When students are given opportunities to talk about books, they improve comprehension by working together to build meaning (Eeds & Wells, 1989). In addition, discussions about texts motivate students to read and make them feel more engaged with reading (Bowers-Campbell, 2011; DeFrance & Fahrenbruck, 2016; Wilfong, 2009). Moreover, the Common Core State Standards for English Language Arts specify that proficient readers are well versed in reading across genres: students are expected to "read and comprehend complex literary and informational texts independently and proficiently" (National Governors Association Center for Best

Practices & Council of Chief State School Officers, 2010, p. 10). Literature circles can support students in meeting this goal, especially if they are implemented continuously throughout the school year.

Much has been written about how teachers can plan and structure literature circles; we direct readers of this book who are especially interested in this topic to Daniels (2002), whose work informs our own understanding. Basically, literature circles are groups of four or five students who meet on a regular basis to discuss a common text. Groups are formed based on interest rather than a student's instructional reading level; students are placed in a group with peers who share a desire to read a particular book. During literature circle meetings, which are held during class time, students lead the discussion, raising their own questions and addressing book-related topics they want to discuss. Sometimes students perform a particular role within their literature circle group. One student might perform the role of "discussion director" and develop and ask questions of group members, and another student may enact the role of "word wizard" and define and explain potentially unfamiliar vocabulary to his, her, or their peers. Other roles may include "literary luminary" (a student who critically examines and shares interesting passages in the text, paying special attention to the writer's craft) and "artful artist" (a student who illustrates a significant scene, a character, or a setting and shares it within the group). Roles rotate within the group, so each student has an opportunity to assume each role. Students may complete a worksheet to scaffold their performance of literature circle roles; we recommend visiting www.readwritethink.org and searching for the *Literature Circles: Getting Started* lesson plan. This website offers free literature circle role sheets that teachers may download and share. However, as Daniels notes, role sheets are intended to be temporary scaffolds for students who are new to literature circles. As students gain more practice with meaningfully discussing books, teachers may dispense with roles and role sheets altogether.

Although literature circles are a student-centered instructional practice, teachers still play a role. When students are new to literature circles, the teacher must model each role and give students feedback as they practice enacting each role. The teacher is also responsible for assessment; though some teachers opt not to grade literature circles, many teachers listen in on students' conversations, assessing students' abilities to keep the conversation on the book, ask questions, disagree respectfully, listen closely, and demonstrate positive social skills. Teachers may take observational notes or use a checklist for this purpose.

Before students gather into small groups for their literature circle meetings, the teacher often teaches a short lesson about discussion procedures or literary elements (Daniels, 2002). In the lesson plan included in this chapter, the teacher scaffolds the making disconnections strategy in a lesson just like Hannah did in the opening vignette of Chapter 8. Because the students in Hannah's classroom are reading different texts in their literature circles, she might model how to make disconnections using a shorter picture book that can be shared in a single class period. In the lesson plan presented in Table 9.1, the teacher uses the book *My Beautiful Birds* to introduce students to the topic of making disconnections.

Table 9.1 Lesson Plan

Central focus: Students will *analyze* how and why their own lives are different from the lives of characters portrayed in a text.	**Subject:** English language arts
Grade: 7	**Classroom context:** Whole class to small group

Standards

CCSS.ELA-LITERACY.SL.7.1: Engage effectively in a range of collaborative discussions (one-on-one, in groups, and teacher-led) with diverse partners on grade 7 topics, texts, and issues, building on others' ideas, and expressing their own clearly.

CCSS.ELA-LITERACY.SL.7.1a: Come to discussions prepared, having read or researched material under study; explicitly draw on that preparation by referring to evidence on the topic, text, or issue to probe and reflect on ideas under discussion.

CCSS.ELA-LITERACY.SL.7.1c: Pose questions that elicit elaboration and respond to others' questions and comments with relevant observations and ideas that bring the discussion back on topic as needed.

Objectives

Students will *know* that making disconnections means considering how one's own life is different from the lives and lived experiences of characters portrayed in a text.

Students will *understand* that making disconnections between their own lives and a text can raise their awareness of real-life inequalities existing among people and groups.

Students will *be able to* analyze differences between their own lives and the lives of characters portrayed in a book by applying the making disconnections strategy in a peer-led discussion of a text.

Assessment: The teacher will observe students as they engage in literature circle discussions; specifically, the teacher will make note of whether students are able to apply the making disconnections strategy. The teacher will use the checklist provided (see Figure 9.1 at the end of this lesson plan) to determine if students have successfully met the objectives of the lesson. If the teacher is unable to assess all students in a single class period, the teacher may continue assessing in subsequent literature circle discussions. In addition, the teacher will collect students' Making Disconnections graphic organizers (see Figure 9.2 at the end of this lesson plan) and review them to determine if students understand how to meaningfully apply the strategy; the teacher will also review the self-reflections that students write in their English-language arts notebooks. Assessment of the discussions, graphic organizers, and self-reflections will help the teacher determine if the students have met the lesson objectives or if the lesson needs to be retaught.

Materials

A Day in the Life video clips: https://www.youtube.com/watch?v=AqpQYeYo0zM
My Beautiful Blackbirds by Suzanne Del Rizzo
Multiple copies of Teacher Checklist (see Figure 9.1; one checklist per student)

(Continued)

Table 9.1   Lesson Plan (Continued)

Multiple copies of Making Disconnections Graphic Organizer (see Figure 9.2; two per student—one for in-class work and one for homework)
Computer and projector (to display Making Connections Graphic Organizer)

Academic language function: Analyze	Language demands: Listening to the teacher read aloud and model the making disconnections strategy, reading a grade-level text, speaking with peers about a text, listening to peers speak about a text, writing ideas on a graphic organizer

Lesson introduction

1. The teacher says, "Today before we meet with in our literature circles, I am going to introduce a new strategy called *making disconnections*. To begin, I am going to show you a short video clip of Okello Preska, a girl who is attending school in Uganda, a country located in the central part of the African continent. The video shows some of the daily activities in her life. As you watch the video, I would like you to make connections between Okello's life and your life. We have practiced this strategy before with books we've read. Additionally, I would like you to think about how your life is *different* from Okello's. We will watch and then discuss what you thought."

2. The teacher plays the video clip and students watch: https://www.youtube.com/watch?v=AqpQYeYo0zM

3. After the clip has played, the teacher asks, "What are some connections you see between your life and Okello's?" The teacher calls on several students to respond. Students might say things such as "Okello goes to school like we do" and "I'm in charge of washing dishes at my house like Okello is at her house."

4. The teacher says, "Now, let's think about the differences between your lives and Okello's life. *How* are your lives different from hers?" The teacher calls on students to respond. They may make observations such as "Okello walks to school and I take the bus," "We have computers and technology in our classroom and Okello's classroom doesn't," and "I have a plastic toothbrush I bought at the store, and Okello uses a stick to brush her teeth."

5. The teacher asks, "*Why* do you think your life is different from Okello's life? What are the reasons for these differences?" Students may respond by saying "Okello lives in a different country" or "Okello's family might be poor." If this happens, the teacher should ask additional probing questions such as "Why do you think the United States is different from Uganda?" and "What are some reasons why Okello's family could be poor?" As the teacher asks these questions, students realize that Uganda may not have as many resources and economic and educational opportunities as the United States; some students may make connections to their world history class by realizing that Uganda's poverty could be related to European colonialism in Africa, a topic the students have studied. When having this discussion, the teacher should be very careful about having students notice that the United States is *different* from Uganda but not superior to Uganda.

6. The teacher says, "You are familiar with the making connections strategy. Making connections can help you better understand the text you are reading. Today, we are going to learn a new strategy called *making disconnections*. When we make disconnections to a text, we think about how we are different from the people in the text and the reasons why. When we talk about these differences, we can learn about the ways that our world is unequal for different people. The purpose of today's lesson is to teach you the making disconnections strategy, and you will have a chance to apply the strategy in today's literature circle meeting."

Instructional input

7. The teacher says, "I am going to model how the making disconnections strategy works. I will read aloud a picture book, *My Beautiful Birds* by Suzanne Del Rizzo, and show you how I make disconnections to this text. This book is another example of contemporary realistic fiction just like you are reading in your literature circles." The teacher begins reading the book, which is about a boy named Sami forced to evacuate his home and live in a refugee camp because of the Syrian civil war. Sami is devastated at leaving behind his home and beloved pet birds.

8. The teacher projects the *Making Connections* graphic organizer (Figure 9.2) so that all students can see it clearly. The teacher says, "I can use this graphic organizer to help me think about my disconnections to this text. First, I need to name a disconnection. I am going to write 'My life is different from Sami's life' in this first box."

9. "What I wrote in the first box is not enough information—it's a vague statement," the teacher says. "I need to explain more about my disconnection. In my second box, I need to explain *how* my life is different from Sami's life. I will write 'Sami lives in a refugee camp. I live in a house' in the second box."

10. The teacher says, "Next, I need to think about *why* my life is different from Sami's. In the third box, I will write 'Sami is from a country where there is a war and people have to leave their homes, and my country does not have a war happening.' I also noticed that Sami's parents don't seem to have jobs, and people need jobs to pay for housing. I'm also going to write 'Sami's parents don't have a job to pay for housing, and I have a job that helps me to pay for my house.'"

11. "The fourth and final box is the most important box," the teacher explains. "Now, I need to ask questions about my *hows* and *whys* that I wrote in my second and third boxes. In my third box, I wrote that Sami lives in a country where there is war, and that is one reason why our lives are different. This leads me to a question: Why do people have to leave home when there is a war? I'm going to write that down in my fourth box. I also wonder what else happens to people's lives when there is a war in their country, so I'm going to write down that question in the box, too. Maybe Sami's parents lost their jobs when their country went to war, and that's why they had to live in a refugee camp instead of moving into another house. As I read about Sami's life, I wondered what would happen if the United States had a civil war like the one in Syria. Here's

(*Continued*)

Table 9.1 Lesson Plan (Continued)

another question I am going to write down: If the United States had a civil war today, what would happen to everyday people?" The teacher writes down the questions in the fourth box and invites students to generate additional questions based on the *hows* and *whys* written on the graphic organizer.
12.   The teacher says, "Let's talk about some of these questions together. Why do you think people like Sami have to leave home when there is a war?" The teacher calls on students to respond, and if time allows, the teacher asks additional questions written in the fourth box of the graphic organizer.
13.   The teacher says, "Thinking about how my life is different from Sami's helped me think about the ways the world is unjust. By making a disconnection, I thought about some questions I had that led us to a conversation about war and how people are hurt when their countries are at war. Although Sami's story is fictional, making disconnections to it helped us understand real-world issues that real people like Sami's family face."

Work session

14. The teacher passes out copies of the Making Disconnections graphic organizer and instructs students to gather in their literature circle groups. (All students in the class are currently placed in a group, and each group is reading a self-selected work of contemporary realistic fiction.)

15. "Before you begin discussing your book, I would like you to take a few minutes to make a disconnection to something you have read in the last few chapters. Write your disconnections and questions on your graphic organizer. When everyone in your group has had a chance to complete the graphic organizer, you may begin your literature circle discussions. Please make sure you share your disconnections and the questions you wrote during your discussion."

16. The students work independently, and as they finish the graphic organizers, they start talking about the chapters they read for homework last night and the disconnections they made with their fellow literature circle group members. Students also discuss the questions they wrote on their graphic organizers stemming from their disconnections. As the students are engaged in conversation, the teacher visits each group for several minutes and uses the assessment checklist (Figure 9.1) to determine if students are meeting the lesson objectives. If students seem to be struggling with making disconnections or talking about the broader social and political issues connected to their disconnections, the teacher should ask questions or supply prompts to scaffold their thinking.

Lesson closure

17. After students have had time to discuss their books, disconnections, and questions in their groups, the teacher calls the attention of the whole class. "The goal of today's lesson was to show you that making disconnections can help you think about why people and groups of people are different. Making disconnections leads us to ask questions about why the world is different and sometimes unfair for different people, and these conversations help us become more critically literature readers," the teacher explains.

18. The teacher asks students to take out their English-language arts notebooks. "Write the date at the top of a new page in your notebook. I would like you to reflect on the making disconnections strategy. How did it go in your group? How comfortable are you with using the strategy? What questions or areas of confusion do you have about the strategy? When you are finished, pass up your notebook and the graphic organizer you completed earlier, and I will collect them."

19. As students complete their self-reflections, the teacher distributes another set of Making Disconnections graphic organizers to each student. "For homework tonight, continue reading your literature circle book. Make at least one disconnection and complete this graphic organizer. Bring it to your literature circle meeting tomorrow."

Differentiation

This lesson plan is differentiated according to interest because students are reading self-selected books in their literature circle groups and making disconnections that relate to their own lives.

Students who require extra support with making disconnections could work one on one with the teacher or with a small group of students in Step 15. The teacher can provide questions or prompts to scaffold students' thinking about the *hows* and *whys* of their disconnections.

Students who need a challenge can be asked to link their disconnections from their literature circle books or *My Beautiful Birds* to topics they have studied in other curricular areas. For example, when considering the question "If the United States had a civil war today, what would happen to everyday people?" (from the teacher's model graphic organizer for *My Beautiful Birds* in Step 11), students could be asked to consider what they learned about the American Civil War of 1861–1865 and consider how the impact of a civil war would differ if it happened in today's world.

Although we present a single lesson plan in this chapter, readers of this book should keep in mind that the teacher may need to model the making disconnections strategy more than once for students to become proficient. Further, this lesson plan assumes that students in the class are already proficient with the routines of literature circles. If teachers are new to using literature circles in the classroom, it will be necessary to model literature circle procedures and how to sustain a text-based conversation before teaching a lesson like this one. Again, we point readers to Daniels (2002) for the purpose of further learning about literature circles.

MODIFYING THE LESSON PLAN

The strategy of making disconnections is a flexible one that can be taught with nearly any book, though it works particularly well when students are reading realistic fiction: it may be easier for students to make connections and disconnections

Student name:

Date:

Book title:

_____ The student made a meaningful disconnection to a character or event in the book.

Comments:

_____ The student explained how his, her, or their own life is different from the character or event to which the student disconnects in the book.

Comments:

_____ The student explained why he, she, or they believe his, her, or their own life is different from the character or event in the book.

Comments:

_____ In response to a peer's or his, her, or their own disconnection, the student asked new questions about the book or social conditions or inequalities addressed in the book.

Comments:

Figure 9.1   Teacher Checklist for Making Disconnections Literature Circle Discussion

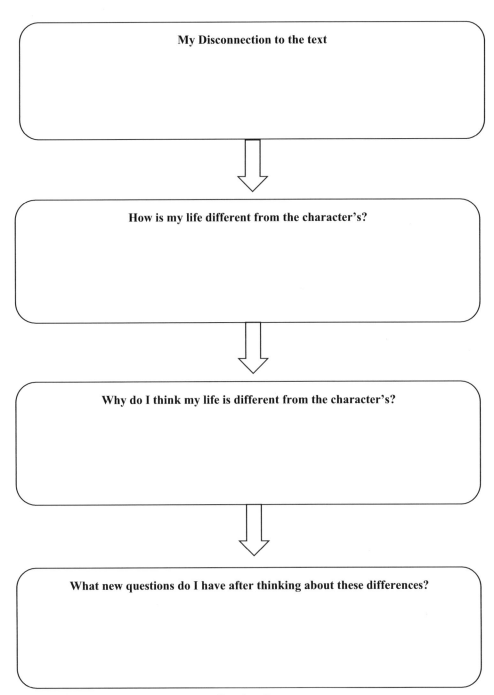

My Disconnection to the text

↓

How is my life different from the character's?

↓

Why do I think my life is different from the character's?

↓

What new questions do I have after thinking about these differences?

Figure 9.2 Making Disconnections Graphic Organizer

when they are reading about contemporary characters and events. However, teachers may choose to teach the strategy by selecting a different video clip in the Lesson Introduction or modeling with a different book during Instructional Input. Teachers should choose sources that align with their students' interests and readiness as well as curricular goals. This lesson plan is written for seventh-grade students, but it can easily be modified for students in lower-grade levels. For instance, before students are asked to independently complete the Making Disconnections graphic organizer, the teacher could place students in their literature circle groups and allow them to complete the graphic organizer together. Then, each group's work could be shared with the whole class. Students could evaluate whether their peers have considered appropriate reasons for their disconnections and written questions based on their disconnections that touch on broader social and political issues. Alternatively, the teacher could provide additional modeling by making additional disconnections to *My Beautiful Birds* using input from students. As stated previously, the process of making disconnections may need to be modeled through teacher think-alouds on multiple occasions before students are ready to utilize the strategy independently.

10

Fantasy

Joe's fourth-grade classroom is all abuzz. This morning they are going to debate whether the frog narrator in Life According to Og the Frog *should remain in the fictional Room 26. Students have been assigned to two different teams. One team is taking the identity of Og, the fictional frog in the book they are reading. They have combed through the book to find examples of how Og, the narrator of the story, has decided he belongs in Room 26 including his growing friendship with Humphrey the hamster who is also a class pet. They talk about his relationships with the students in the class, their teacher, and her husband. The other team is taking the identity of Og the real frog. They also draw heavily from the text of the book, particularly the words of the visiting scientist about the needs of frogs. They plan to point out the issues of Og remaining in the classroom over a weekend or a holiday and what happens to Og when the power goes off. "Does Og have enough space?" they ask, pointing to a scene where his swimming area is increased. One student has asked what will happen to a class pet over the summer and then when a new group of students return the next year. Two of the students ask to visit the library to ask the librarian to help them research wild frogs as pets. The debate culminates a novel study conducted in this classroom that has focused on identity and how the author has created characters in this book including the students in the classroom, their teacher, her husband who is in a wheelchair, a visiting female scientist, and another class pet, the hamster. Students have been charting the character traits of each and exploring how the author has used the element of fantasy to allow Og, the frog, to serve as an observer who tells us about these identities. Joe hopes his students have an understanding now about the difference between realistic elements and fantasy in this fictional chapter book. In particular, he wants them to think about the role of a talking frog in providing key observations about the identities in a classroom of diverse students. Chapter 11 describes approaches that teachers can take to teach this or a similar lesson.*

DEFINING FANTASY

Fantasy, by definition, includes magic or other elements that are not possible in the physical world. Such stories have been around for a long time as evidenced by the magical elements in many folk and fairy tales. In fantasy, animals may talk or otherwise act as people, or a tree may narrate a story from its stationary point of view. Fantastical characters such as elves, fairies, mermaids, or extraterrestrials populate the story, or entire imaginary worlds and settings have been created by the author. Fantasy has several subgenres or related genres such as magical realism where an element of magic exists along with the everyday reality. High fantasy often includes struggles between good and evil and thus deals ultimately with topics of social justice. Historical fantasy provides an opportunity to reexamine history through a different perspective. *Dactyl Hill Squad* set in New York City in 1863 during the Civil War features dinosaurs serving as transportation, weapons, and allies in the fight for justice in an action-packed fantasy with elements of historical fiction.

Fiction set in the future as either science fiction or dystopian fiction may explore the future consequences of social and/or political decisions about the environment or control of individuals. A fantastical setting, characters, or plot may allow for exploration of social issues from an outside perspective or from a perspective that puts distance between current political situations or personalities. For example, in *Wishtree* the tree's long life and wisdom provide a different narrator for a tale of prejudice and ecological consequence. The imaginary friend in *Crenshaw*, a giant cat with that name, offers humor and insight into the heavy issues of homelessness and poverty. Animals narrating stories such as *Life According to Og the Frog* provide observations in a classroom about the struggles of human children dealing with foster care or immigration from an empathetic, outside perspective.

Fantasy is a popular genre with many young readers. Fantasy may offer a type of escape immersing readers in an imaginary time and place with fantastic adventures. Often young people are the protagonists who possess special powers or abilities. Numerous popular series including Harry Potter and The Hunger Games have garnered a following of adult readers and inspired movie versions.

EVALUATING FANTASY

Evaluation of fantasy includes the development of a believable and consistent fantastical world, characters, or actions. The unbelievable must be believable within the pages of the story. A book may be realistic except for an element of fantasy such as an imaginary friend, talking animals, or a special power the character possesses. Or the author may have created an entire world with a separate language, setting, social identities, and norms. Evaluating this type of "world building" is an aspect of evaluating this kind of fantasy. How thoroughly does the author immerse us in the imaginary world? In this type of fantasy we look for rich descriptions and language. Are there inconsistencies in the descriptions? Readers may find themselves asking "Is this real?" as with the giant talking cat, Crenshaw.

Children are known to have imaginary friends, and the reader looks for evidence that Crenshaw is more than a figment of Jackson's imagination. In *The Midnight War of Mateo Martinez*, Mateo is not sure whether he has imagined skunks stealing his bicycle until he explores the evidence and eventually finds corroboration as a friend and younger sister also interact with the talking skunks.

Enchantment and fantasy have deep roots in cultural storytelling and are often features of folk and fairy tales. These stories may have included fantastical characters, magic, and "once-upon-a-time" settings, but they also often conveyed cultural values and norms with lessons for young listeners. Evaluating modern fantasy may include questioning familiar tropes from traditional literature such as witches or talking animals. How has the author used these to good or bad effect? Fantasy authors may reimagine a common fairytale as in *The Rat Prince*, a retelling of Cinderella featuring royal and magical rats. *Aru Shah and the End of Time* introduces Indian mythology as two young girls prove themselves to be heroines as they journey through the Kingdom of Death with courage and humor.

Good and evil may be starkly contrasted in fantasy leading toward a discussion of whether the characters are truly one or the other or simply misunderstood. In *Mars Evacuees*, Morrors are presented as monsters who have taken over Earth and now threaten Mars until four children capture one and grow to understand what has driven the Morrors to Earth. They discover the Morror they have captured is a child like they are and part of a complex family life and culture. Such examples can lead readers to consider how we may characterize cultures that we don't understand as dangerous unless we take the time to learn about them. In *Mars Evacuees* it is the children who help the adult world understand common interests between the two cultures to save Earth and the solar system.

Many titles in the fantasy genre are lengthy and may belong to a series with multiple volumes, for example, <u>Harry Potter</u>. Aficionados of the genre love the length and investment of time, allowing readers to be immersed in the world. A longer book allows for the fullest creation of the fantasy, and multiple volumes in a series allow the author to continue building on the creative investment of developing a fantastical world. In the classroom, it may be difficult to find the time for these lengthy titles from multi-part series. However, the genre with its action-packed plots, heroic characters, and deeds often captivates readers to independently complete the book or series.

READING FANTASY WITH A CRITICAL LITERACY LENS

Fantasy is an effective vehicle for critical literacy. As a genre, fantasy, by definition, disrupts the commonplace (Lewison, Flint, & Van Sluys, 2002), for example, through talking animals, magic, or imaginary worlds and times. Fantasy for young readers usually features young characters courageously taking action for a better world such as through encounters with demons in *Aru Shah and the End of Time*, communicating with dinosaurs in *Dactyl Hill Squad*, or helping a witch to save dragons in *Dragons in a Bag*.

All kinds of fantasy provide excellent examples of the power of words to create worlds, which is an ultimate tenet of critical literacy to read the word and the world. Drawing the attention of readers to the skills employed by authors to create believable worlds leads us to understand how all language can be employed to build a world. Often in fantasy the author will develop a new language or names providing the opportunity to talk about the power of language and names. How do we in our everyday use of naming create meaning? It's a familiar trope in fantasy, for example, not to let anyone know one's true name because it gives them a type of power over the individual. Willa in *Willa of the Wood* worries about this when Nathaniel asks for her name. Communication is often a barrier to be overcome in fantasy where animals talk but are not understood by people, or the tree in *Wishtree* tries to find a way to communicate with people.

Discussions of fantasy provide an opportunity to talk about discerning truth from fabrication in today's media and politics. Fantasy also allows for deep discussion about how we know something is real or not and could therefore lead to critical discussions about propaganda or fake news and the importance of discerning what is true from what is not true. Readers could be asked what elements of the story might be true and what elements are clearly not true and why. There may be an entirely imaginative world and characters where the relationships, particularly those related to power, ring true, and students could be asked to think about examples in their own lives. Imagining the consciousness of animals or trees may allow readers to question their taken-for-granted treatment of other living things.

A hallmark of fantasy is imagination. Critical literacy asks that we imagine other possible social and cultural worlds, and fantasy is perfectly suited to this purpose. Critical literacy may demand that we think about the future consequences of what we take for granted, whether it's our use of resources of water, fossil fuels, or green space or relationships of power. Fantasy may recast these problems into made-up worlds or future worlds. In a fantastical world, an issue may become a core concern. Time travel into the past or ghosts from the past to inhabit the present allow us to think about the historical antecedents of present social and cultural contexts. Imagination is not just about negative consequences but can include imagining better alternatives or futures for ourselves.

Fantasy may reward "good" behavior and thoughts while eventually punishing greed, violence, or misuse of power. In *Bluecrowne*, Lucy is told to steal a magical knife in order to get her brother who has been kidnapped by a time-traveler and a

---

Sidebar 10.1   Question Stems for Fantasy

- What social and cultural norms exist in this fantasy?
- Who has power in the story?
- How is power challenged in the story?
- What parallels are there between the story and current events?

conflagrationist for his powers with fireworks. In an encounter with the smith who created the knife, Lucy is told why he will not sell the knife because the person who asked for it saw it as a weapon of destruction that could tear out someone's throat. Instead, the smith offers it to Lucy for the taking as her motives are more positive, but she also foresees the violent use of the knife even if it saves her brother and does not accept it.

Fantasy has been critiqued for a lack of diverse characters (Baker, 2007; Obeso, 2014) and a predominance of Western European settings despite its focus on otherness. Several newer fantasy titles offer readers a glimpse into other cultures through the inclusion of diverse characters. In *Bluecrowne*, Lucy's half brother and his mother are both of Chinese descent. In *The Gauntlet* the protagonist Farrah wears a hijab scarf and talks about her family's connections to the Muslim country of Bangladesh. While Farrah and her friends venture into a game-based world that is clearly fantastical, there are numerous references to foods, holidays, and practices of her family as well as times when she remembers being teased at school for being different. Inside the Gauntlet game, Farrah and her friends battle an autocratic Timekeeper who holds the residents hostage to his sandstorm rages, and they are befriended by a resistance comprised of a gang of lizards. In this classic battle of good versus evil, when the identity of the Timekeeper is revealed, Farrah feels empathy for the character and worries about his well-being. In *Willa of the Wood*, we are told the protagonist has green skin and also the power to blend into her surroundings and change color.

Social issues find themselves into the worlds of fantasy. In *Bayou Magic*, the oil industry in the Gulf of Mexico threatens the people and the wildlife in the area. With the help of mermaids, Maddy saves the bayou from disaster. In *Mars Evacuees*, questions about gender identity arise when one of the characters is a captured Morror, who is asked "Are you a he or a she" and answers "neither" because Morrors have five genders (it takes three to reproduce) and so the children from Earth decide to refer to the character as "they." A basic premise of the book is that Earth has been taken over by Morrors, who initially only wanted to colonize the poles and promised to reverse global warming on Earth. *Mars Evacuees* also challenges stereotypes, with the strong female characters trained to be soldiers in the battle to save Earth and the solar system. An urban setting is featured in *Dragons in a Bag*, where a young boy, Jax, ventures to return small dragons to their magical world as his mother struggles to prevent their eviction.

In *Life According to Og the Frog* readers are provided an opportunity to see an everyday classroom from the outside perspective of the class pet. Through Og's observations, the reader learns about other students, the teacher, and the custodian. The character of Og, a wild animal held captive in an aquarium, also raises questions debated within the story about the ethical treatment of animals. An important conflict within the book is between the wild animal, a frog, and the imaginary Og who develops an identity as a member of the classroom with emotional connections to many of the human characters in the story. In the introductory lesson featured in Chapter 11, the teacher builds a foundation for understanding the fantasy elements of the story and the questions engendered about wild animals in captivity.

ANNOTATED BIBLIOGRAPHY

Applegate, Katherine. *Crenshaw*. 2015. 243 pp. Feiwel and Friends. 978125004328
> Entering fifth grade, Jackson has a seemingly imaginary friend, a giant surfboarding cat named Crenshaw who shows up at key moments to provide lighthearted relief from the struggles of Jackson's family with poverty and homelessness.

Applegate, Katherine. *Wishtree*. 2017. Santoso, Charles. 215 pp. Feiwel and Friends. 9781250043221
> Narrated by a tree where people annually tie their wishes. Observes a newcomer in the neighborhood whose family is Muslim. Treated with indifference and fear but also outright prejudice when "leave" is carved in the tree's bark. The narrator is a calm and optimistic observer who decided to intervene. Subtle about the differences and heartwarmingly unsubtle about welcome and unity.

Barnhill, Kelly. *The Girl Who Drank the Moon*. 2016. 386 pp. Algonquin Young Readers. 9781616205676
> Controlled by their fear of the witch in the forest, the people of the Protectorate offer a child sacrifice each year. The witch rescues the abandoned babies, and one, Luna, ingests moonlight and grows to have magical powers. A classic and multilayered struggle between evil and love.

Beatty, Robert. *Willa of the Wood*. 2018. 376 pp. Disney Hyperion. 9781368005845
> Green-skinned Willa is a thief in the night stealing for her Faeren people and their leader the padaran who fears and mistrusts the settlers in the Smoky Mountains until she is befriended by one and learns to question the cruel and dark side of the society where she has belonged.

Birney, Betty G. *Life According to Og the Frog*. 2018. 150 pp. G. P. Putnam's Sons. 9781524739942
> Og the frog is a class pet in room 26 whose narration details his adjustment to life in a tank and observations about the variety of students and their teacher.

Chokshi, Roshani. *Aru Shah and the End of Time*. 2018. 355 pp. Disney Hyperion. 978136801235-5
> Twelve-year-old Aru lights a lamp and releases the demon Sleeper. In an action- and humor-packed tale, she and her sidekick, Mini, must set the world right. Characters and stories from Hindu mythology infuse the compelling story.

Citro, Asia. *Zoey and Sassafras: Dragons and Marshmallows.* 2017. 96 pp. Lindsay, Marion. Innovation Press. 9781943147090
In this series, the young protagonist is a Black girl with an interest in scientific observation. Like her mother, Zoey has a talent for helping injured animals who come to her for help. One day a sick baby dragon shows up, and Zoey must discover how to help it. This series is written for third and fourth graders; it is a transitional-type novel with numerous illustrations and could be a quick-class or small-group read.

Elliott, Zetta. *Dragons in a Bag.* B, Geneva. 2018. 154 pp. Random House. 9781524770457
When his mother must go to court to avoid eviction from their home, Jaxon is left with an old woman he discovers is a witch. She enlists his help in rescuing a pair of baby dragons.

Hargrave, Kiran Millwood. *The Cartographer's Daughter.* 2016. 224 pp. Knopf Book for Young Readers. 9780553535280
Isabella, a mapmaker's daughter, draws on her knowledge of maps to lead a group into the forbidden forest and rescue the community from a harsh ruling family. Published in paperback as *The Girl of Ink and Stars.*

Hodder, Bridget. *The Rat Prince.* 2016. 260 pp. Farrar, Straus and Giroux. 9780374302139
In alternating chapters, Char, the rat prince, and Cinderella retell the familiar story complete with royal intrigue and magic.

McDougall, Sophia. *Mars Evacuees.* 2015. 404 pp. Harper. 9780062294005
Twelve-year-old Alice Dare is chosen to evacuate to Mars because Earth is threatened by aliens and climate change. She worries about her mother, a spacefighter, busy battling the alien Morrors, but her adventure on the planet Mars is also threatened by alien strife. Strong female protagonist and challenging encounters with surprising aliens provide a thought-provoking, often humorous tale of adventure.

Milford, Kate. *Bluecrowne: A Greenglass House Story.* Wong, Nicole. 2018. 245 pp. Clarion Books. 9781328466884
Lucy Bluecrowne lives in an enchanted house with her father, his Chinese wife, and her half brother whose talent for pyrotechnics makes him a target for a pair of villains. Infused with Chinese folklore, time travel, and an intelligent protagonist determined to save her brother.

Older, Daniel Jose. *Dactyl Hill Squad.* 2018. 256 pp. Arthur A. Levine/Scholastic. 9781338168812
Dinosaurs serve as transport in 1860s New York City as Civil War rages and draft riots erupt in the city. A likeable female protagonist demonstrates bravery and an unusual ability to communicate with the reptilian giants in this mash-up of fantasy and historical fiction.

Pennypacker, Sara. *Pax.* Klassen, J. 2016. 288 pp. Balzer + Bray. 9780062377012
In anguish over the decision to release his pet fox, Pax, into the wild, Peter runs away to find his beloved pet. Meanwhile, Pax must survive in the wild where he meets other foxes and must learn to navigate life in a war zone. The story explores the impact of war on families, the environment, and wildlife.

Rhodes, Jewell Parker. *Bayou Magic.* 2015. 235 pp. Little, Brown. 9780316224840
Visiting with her grandmother in the bayou, Maddy learns her family's magical past. When the bayou is threatened by an oil accident and spill, Maddy enlists the help of ancient mermaids to protect the land and those who live there.

Riazi, Karuna. *The Gauntlet.* 2017. 294 pp. Salaam Reads/Simon & Schuster. 9781481486965
Twelve-year-old Farah and two friends enter a mysterious board game and learn they must complete several challenges to escape the game. Mideastern culture mixes with a steampunk flair.

Yardi, Robin. *The Midnight War of Mateo Martinez*. 2016. 173 pp. Carolrhoda. 9781467783064

Mateo witnesses a pair of skunks who steal his old trike. He decides to get to the truth of the situation and protect his neighborhood. Themes of bullying, immigration, and power relations (skunks vs. raccoons) are present in the story.

11

Unpacking Social Identities and Norms through Character Study (Lesson Plan)

Authors of fantasy must create believable social worlds complete with social identities and norms. These identities may be expressed through both main and supporting characters. Williams (2014) discusses the use of animal characters in international books for very young children and the freedom they provide for social commentary. Unpacking characters and how the author develops a character is an appropriate activity for upper elementary children, allowing them to consider the identities and norms an author assigns to characters in a book. These allow students to think about different identities a character may have within the same story—for example as a sibling/child in a family and as a student in a classroom. Sometimes these identities are in conflict and provide impetus for the plot or theme of the story. A recurring theme in *Willa of the Wood*, for example, is the identity of being an "I" or an individual versus the identity of "us" in the group of Faeran where Willa is a member. "There is no I only Us" is a familiar refrain that Willa struggles against as she finds her values at odds with those imposed on the group by their leader. A teacher may guide students to think about their own multiple identities, including gender, age, ethnicity, roles in the classroom, or roles within their family.

In the scenario that opens Chapter 10, we saw Joe's classroom of fourth graders preparing to reenact the debate in *Life According to Og the Frog* about where Og should live. Joe has prepared his students for this culminating activity through character study from the very first pages of the book. This first lesson comparing the characteristics of Og as imaginary and Og as a real frog provide the foundation for understanding the difference between fantasy and facts about frogs.

An animal character that talks allows the author to introduce social identities through the perspective of an outsider. Students may be invited to consider the character of Og and what social identities and norms he reflects. Og has an identity in the classroom as the class pet—What norms follow from this identity? What do the other characters expect from Og and how do they negotiate his position— including the debate about whether to return Og to the wild? Some of the characters to consider may include the teacher, her husband (confined to a wheelchair), the janitor (going back to school), the scientist (a woman), and the student identities in the classroom. How does Og's point of view position the reader to view these characters?

Joe is aware that fourth graders may still need guidance to understand the characteristics of the fantasy genre. Joe's students may have experience with class pets. Og the Frog is a pet in a very realistic school classroom, and Joe plans to lead his students to separate the fantasy from the realistic elements in this story. In this lesson, Joe allows students to uncover the clues within the first pages of the book that indicate that fantasy is the genre. Joe uses character study and a discussion about identity to allow students to uncover how an author develops the identity of a character. For example, the author directly tells us that Og has green skin with black polka dots, but the reader is left to infer that Og is male. While Og is one of the first characters we meet, the story is rich in characters observed by Og, including students, the teacher and her husband, a custodian who longs to become a teacher, and other visitors to the classroom. This first lesson is focused on Og, the main character, and the lesson provides a foundation for additional character study as students complete the book.

Joe also recognizes that this book is an opportunity for students to reflect on their own identities within the classroom as well as outside the classroom. He begins the lesson with an activity where students introduce themselves to a partner as a way of thinking about identity characteristics. This lesson and book might be appropriate for a teacher to use early in the school year where students are unfamiliar with one another. In particular students could complete the Identity Worksheet (see Figure 11.1) about themselves or about a partner they interview.

In this lesson, the teacher reads aloud the first few pages of the book while students read along. This provides an even start for all students in the classroom as they literally begin together on the same page. The teacher can also take this opportunity to explain the use of italics and other fonts in this text to show when the character is dreaming, making noise, or singing. The author introduces both real and imaginary characteristics of the main character within the first few pages. The teacher can model the difference between those that are explicit and those the reader can infer.

Authors often position characters and their identities as much through what is not explicitly stated as what must be inferred by the reader. Understanding these constructions is one of the important skills in critical literacy. In particular, in this lesson, students are asked to view the text from multiple perspectives (Lewison, Flint, & Van Sluys, 2002; McLaughlin & DeVoogd, 2004) as they analyze the perspective of Og, the wild animal, versus Og, the author's fictional character who sings songs and narrates the story about Room 11. The lesson provides a foundation for students to begin talking back to the text as they analyze the author's point of view in constructing an identity for Og, a wild animal. Through Og, readers also see different perspectives about students and staff in a typical elementary school, including a custodian who aspires to be a teacher and students who struggle with family issues and other differences. Finally, the story raises questions regarding social and political issues, such as the ethics of wild animals in captivity and whether they should be returned to the wild.

Table 11.1   Lesson Plan

Central focus: Students will *infer* elements of fantasy and fact from the author's description of a character within the text.	**Subject:** English language arts
Grade: 4	**Classroom context:** Whole class/partners

Standards

CCSS.ELA-Literacy.RL.4.1
Refer to details and examples in a text when explaining what the text says explicitly and when drawing inferences from the text.
CCSS.ELA-Literacy.RL.4.3
Describe in depth a character, setting, or event in a story or drama, drawing on specific details in the text (e.g., a character's thoughts, words, or actions).
CCSS.ELA-Literacy.RL.4.6
Compare and contrast the point of view from which different stories are narrated, including the difference between first- and third-person narrations.

Objectives

Students will *know* how to draw on specific details stated or inferred from the text, such as the character's thoughts, words, and actions, to analyze the identity of the main character.

Students will *understand* that authors use explicit statements as well as clues that must be inferred when constructing a character's identity.

Students will *be able to* contrast the elements of fantasy in *Og the Frog* with the realistic elements of the story using examples from the text.

Assessment: The teacher circulates in the classroom when partners are working on the Identity Worksheet (Figure 11.1) to observe participation by both partners. During the whole class sharing, the teacher will ensure that each partner pair contributes to the whole class chart. The teacher will assess individual completion of the Identity Worksheet (see Figure 11.1 at the end of this lesson plan) with the fantasy characteristics circled.

Materials: Copies of *Life According to Og the Frog* for every student in the class
Identity Worksheets (one for each student to be completed with a partner)
Chart paper and markers

Academic language function: *Infer*	**Language demands:** Listening to the teacher read aloud and following along; attending to the meaning of different fonts in a written text; reading a grade-level text, speaking with peers about a text, listening to peers speak about a text, and writing ideas on a graphic organizer

Lesson introduction

1. The teacher says, "Today we are going to begin reading a new book and learn about how an author develops the identity of a character in a story. Let's start by thinking about the meaning of identity."

(Continued)

Table 11.1   Lesson Plan (Continued)

2.   "If you were new in this class or introducing yourself to someone who was new in this class, think about what you would tell us about yourself. How would you answer the question, *who am I*? You might share something about your family or where you live. You might tell about some of your favorite things, what you like about school, or maybe what you don't like. Take a moment and think about how you would introduce yourself." The teacher allows students a few moments of independent "think time."

3.   "Today we will be working with partners. Turn to the person next to you and introduce yourself to them." Students are given several minutes to talk with a partner. As the conversations wind down, the teacher moves forward.

4.   The teacher asks, "What kinds of things did you include in your introduction? These are all examples of our 'identity' or how we would answer the question *who am I*?" The teacher calls on several students to share.

5.   The teacher reminds students about the definition of fiction: that it is the creation of the author. The teacher says, "One of the things an author of fiction does is create identities for the characters in the story. Did you tell your partner everything about yourself? You didn't have time, right?"

6.   The teacher explains, "An author builds the identity of a character throughout the book. Sometimes the author tell us directly, for example, that a character has brown eyes, but other times we have to follow the clues. We are going to learn about the ways an author tells us about the identity of a character as we read this book."

Instructional input

7.   The teacher holds up a copy of the book *Life According to Og the Frog* displaying the cover and says, "We are going to start a new book today that we will read together as a whole class, *Life According to Og the Frog*, by Betty Birney. Already we know something about Og. Og is a. . . ." The teacher waits for students to say "frog."

8.   The teacher distributes copies of the book to everyone in the class. "What do you notice about the cover? Where do you think this story takes place?" The students share responses. Students should identify clues from the cover that this book is a school story that features a frog. The cover illustration might lead them to wonder if the frog comes to school in someone's backpack. They might also see the picture of a hamster.

9.   The teacher elicits whether anyone is familiar with the books about Humphrey, the hamster featured in a series by the author, and shares that the Humphrey books are about a class pet who writes poetry, suggesting students might want to look for these books in the school's library. The teacher thinks aloud, "Hmmm, I wonder if Og the Frog is in the same classroom as Humphrey and how he gets there."

10.   "Today we are going to begin this book and I am going to begin by reading aloud while you read along in your own copy." The teacher directs students to open their copies of the book and points out the list of twelve books about Humphrey under the heading, "For more adventures in Room 26, look for these titles."

11. The teacher begins by having students turn to the title page. "Remember this is the title page of the book where we will find the title but also the author and the name of the publisher of the book." The teacher reads aloud each of these.

12. The teacher then turns to the "Contents" page. The teacher says, "We don't always see a table of contents in a book of fiction, so this provides an interesting preview of the book."

13. Chapter 1 is entitled "My Leap into Room 26." The teacher asks, "Who do you think is telling this story?" Students may guess it's the frog, and the teacher laughingly asks "But I thought Betty Birney was the author of this book," provoking a discussion about how the author may choose to tell the story from the point of view of a character who tells the story.

14. The teacher shares that this is called using the "first person" to tell the story. "When you introduced yourself earlier in the lesson when you talked with your partner, you used the first person by starting the sentence with 'I' or 'my.'"

15. "What do you think we can learn by having the frog tell the story?" Allow time for some responses. "So we may find out some things about the identity of the frog as he uses the first person."

16. The teacher shows a copy of the Identity Worksheet. "Maybe we can learn some of these things." The teacher models writing the name of the character Og. "Oh we already know, 'I am a frog,'" and the teacher fills out the first line.

17. "Let's find out more about Og; turn the page to the first chapter and follow along as I read."

18. The teacher reads aloud the first three pages of Og up through his song while students follow along in their own books. Some of the important features of this text to point out to students are the use of various fonts to show Og's daydreams and songs and the sounds made by Og and the hamster in the classroom.

19. The teacher points out an early example about a cricket written in italics, *"Now all I have to do is grab it with my great, long tongue and flick it back into my mouth and YUM!"* and thinks aloud about what this tells us about the character: "It has a 'great long tongue' we are told directly. It likes to eat crickets—how do we know that? We can infer it because the author told us it was a cricket and the character said 'yum' after it went in its mouth. So we could finish the sentence on the Identity Worksheet to say 'I like to eat crickets.'"

20. After reading Og's song, the teacher says, "OK, this is where we are going to stop. We have read less than four pages, but I already think we know a lot about the identity of Og. I am going to ask you and your partner to work together to find the clues in the text that tell us or allow us to infer some of the characteristics of Og."

Work session

21. The teacher says, "I am going to give each of you a copy of the Identity Worksheet. Be sure to put your name on the top. You will be working with a partner to find as many answers as possible. You should go back to the text. How many answers can you find on the first page, the second, and so on. I have the first two sentences completed on my worksheet that we found on the first page." Show students how to determine that the first page is page one and write that next to the response.

(Continued)

Table 11.1 Lesson Plan (Continued)

22.	"You may want to start on page one and go through the text to find as many answers as possible. You might find other answers to complete the sentence, 'I am' and 'I like.' Record the page number so we can go back to the text to find the clues for each characteristic."
23.	Allow time for partners to complete the worksheet. The teacher may walk around to observe active participation by all students.
24.	Once partners have completed their worksheets, the teacher asks for partners to share some of their responses. Following each response, the teacher directs a conversation pointing back to the text. The teacher may pose questions such as follows: "Where did you find that in the text? Did the author tell us directly, or did you have to infer it?"
25.	The teacher asks, "Are there parts of Og's identity that you and your partner found that are true for real frogs?" The teacher takes a few responses such as Og is an amphibian and is green with black spots.
26.	The teacher asks if students found some characteristics that are not real and asks partners to look at their Identity Worksheets and circle any characteristics they wrote that are not true for real frogs.
27.	The teacher asks for examples that were not true for real frogs. Several students are called on to share.
28.	The teacher reminds students who is telling us the story in this book. Students will respond "Og the Frog." The teacher asks if frogs tell stories or write books and reminds students of the definition of fiction: the author made the story up, and Og is the creation of Betty Birney. The author chose to make Og the narrator even though this could not really happen.
29.	The teacher introduces the students to two charts: one is Og the real frog, and one is Og the narrator. The teacher asks partners to provide characteristics for Og the narrator by sharing the made-up characteristics they circled on their worksheet and for the real frog with the characteristics they did not circle. These responses are recorded on the correct chart: Realistic Frog or Fantasy Frog.

Lesson closure

30.	The teacher explains, "Sometimes authors create more than one identity for a character. In fiction, an author often uses real-life characteristics such as these." The teacher points out the characteristics that were highlighted as true for real frogs.
31.	"This book is a type of fiction called fantasy because the author has also given Og characteristics that are not real." The teacher points to this chart.
32.	"As we read this book together, we will continue to add to these two charts and think about why the author created these two identities."

Differentiation: Students may be paired strategically to represent different abilities. For example, a striving reader may be supported by being paired with an advanced reader. Students who need writing or language support might be asked to draw pictures showing the characteristics of Og.

Complete each sentence for the character:

Completed by:
_____

| I am |
| I like |
| I dislike |
| I am good at |
| I am proud of |
| I fear |
| I wonder |
| I wish |

Figure 11.1 Identity Worksheet

MODIFYING THE LESSON PLAN

On the surface, *Life According to Og the Frog* is light reading appropriate for elementary grades, but on further examination, the text is rich with opportunities to teach reading strategies and discuss social issues and identities. While an overall theme of the book is a debate about animals in captivity, the book also touches lightly on issues such as immigration, disability, and gender. In this lesson, students begin to understand how an author creates a character both through explicit description and through more subtle clues that require the reader to make inferences about the social identities of a character. In the upper grades, this strategy of unpacking the social identities of a character can be applied to more complex texts. Fantasy is an appropriate genre for such character study because the imaginary characters often disrupt the commonplace. Critical literacy would also ask the reader to think about what is taken for granted or promoted by the author as normal even within a fantastical story. Extensions of this lesson could lead to the scenario presented in Chapter 10 where students use the examples they have collected to debate whether Og the Frog should remain in the classroom taking a position as either the real or the invented frog. Following the debate, students could be given the chance to reflect on their own opinions about a wild animal as a class pet.

12

Picture Books

Maria, an eighth-grade social studies teacher, joins her class in the school library. The librarian, Philip, is reading The Journey, *a picture book, to Maria's class. Philip first asks the students to look at the cover and think about the meaning of the title and the image. What is this book about? What additional information is provided about the book in the illustration on the cover? What is the mood of the book suggested by this cover? From whose point of view is the illustration? From whose view do they expect this book will be told from? "Today," he suggests, "as I read this book and share the images with you, I would like you to think about who is included in the pictures? Who is not in the picture? From whose point of view are we seeing the pictures? Are a variety of perspectives provided in this book?"*

After reading the book to the class, Philip asks the students to open up a Google document he has created to find their assigned small group and discussion role. He has worked with their teacher, Maria, to assign each group a particularly powerful image from the book as part of the prompt. Students are then encouraged to respond to the image from their assigned role. Philip is using visual literacy and an asynchronous discussion strategy to ask students to think critically about the presentation of a topic through images. Visual literacy is increasingly recognized as an important component of literacy as viewers create meaning from images, not only texts. Given the wide use of images in social media, advertisement, television, and films, a literate person needs to think critically about who created the image, for what audience, and with what intention? Picture books offer an excellent resource for teaching visual literacy. Chapter 13 presents a lesson plan that librarians or teachers can utilize to achieve this purpose.

DEFINING PICTURE BOOKS

The Caldecott Medal, awarded since 1939, defines a picture book as "one that essentially provides the child with a visual experience. A picture book has a collective unity of story-line, theme, or concept, developed through the series of pictures of which the book is comprised" (Association of Library Services to Children, 2008). While only one book is awarded the medal in a given year, there may also be several honor books. By definition, a picture book is a blend of pictures and text in which the pictures are responsible for conveying a significant portion of the meaning of the book. Picture books are compact, often thirty-two or forty-eight pages, and therefore shareable within a class period. Some are quite sophisticated in the style of illustration, the topics addressed, and the potential for layered interpretations. Picture books are often overlooked for use with older students, but they are very accessible, and their apparent simplicity can be unpacked to reveal deeper levels of meaning. The Caldecott criteria define their audience as up to and including age fourteen, and therefore, older students are in the scope of this award. The Caldecott Award is one place to look for potential titles to use in a classroom, and the criteria may help identify other worthy titles published in a given year.

Wordless picture books, in particular, offer the opportunity to explore how a plot or character unfolds visually. Turn the pages in *Wolf in the Snow*, by Matthew Cordell, and the story unfolds like a film as a young girl is lost walking home from school in the snow. Alternating full-page spreads show a young wolf separated from the pack. Astute viewers will notice the young girl facing right, while the wolves are facing left foreshadowing their encounter. We see the girl and wolf cub up close as they find each other, and then in a wide double-spread, they look very small against the expansive, snowy spread. With the girl's assistance, the cub and pack are reunited while the young girl still struggles through the snow. Distant searchlights show someone is searching for her and circling wolves aid the rescue. While this is a deceptively simple story to be appreciated by even very young children, it opens the opportunity to talk about distrust between groups, in this case wolves and people, and how a universal concern for the young can unite their efforts.

Picture books address a diversity of themes, including those familiar to young children such as family, friendship, and school, but there are also picture books that introduce readers to other times and places and some with overt themes related to social justice. Their variety offers teachers and librarians openings to topics for older students, including difficult topics in families or school such as divorce, unemployment, relationships, bullying, and dealing with differences. Time and place in picture books may lead to historical and global explorations, again not necessarily in easy ways. War, immigration, and government control feature in some picture book treatments. In this chapter we will introduce some of those titles, among others, featured in the annotated bibliography. Eve Bunting, Jeanette Winter, and Patricia Polacco are three authors who often address tough social topics.

EVALUATING PICTURE BOOKS

Picture books are a form that includes several recognizable features. It's helpful to provide students with the vocabulary to talk about these features beginning with the book's cover and/or jacket. Some picture books are designed with a different image on the cover and jacket. For example, *Town Is by the Sea*, by Joanne Schwartz, has a young boy on the cover looking over a small town and out to sea; sunlight ripples over the water. Take a peek under the jacket and discover the same vista with a setting or rising sun over the water and darkened town without the boy. The book jacket wraps the cover with flaps on the inside; students may be familiar with using these to preview the book's content and learn about the author and illustrator. Endpapers are the first and last pages of the book affixed to the book's covers and may or may not be decorated. Even solid colored endpapers may serve to set the mood or tone of the book comparing a dark, charcoal to sunny yellows in another presentation. The shape and orientation of a book are also intentional design choices to share with students. A wide rectangle opens to very wide double-spreads in *Town Is by the Sea* that are sometimes broken into smaller frames such as the opening with the young boy swinging across the page, "We go so far I can see far out to sea," and a few pages later, the full opening shows a dark sea with men working in a thin strip at the bottom, "And deep down under that sea, my father is digging for coal." Compare this wide rectangle shape to a tall rectangle such as *The Rooster Who Would Not Be Quiet!* that emphasizes the upright, proud, and tall rooster on the cover. It's also interesting to note when a book changes the orientation of the pages as in *Drum Dream Girl* where a turn of the book changes a wide orientation to a very tall one, or a book like *Malala/Iqbal* that features two stories: one about Malala and one about a boy, Iqbal. Read one and then flip the book to read the other. The two stories meet in a middle spread. This design choice emphasizes their parallel and interconnected stories.

When it comes to evaluating picture books, a language of art critique is helpful. The teacher or librarian might collaborate with an art teacher to lead such a discussion. An artist may work in a variety of media, including paint, pencil, ink, collage, photography, computer generated, or a mixture employing multiple media. Paint includes oil, acrylic, watercolor and gouache. Often, the medium is described on the back of the title page or on the book jacket flap. The snowy *Wolf in the Snow* has a hush rendered in watercolor and pen and ink and might be compared to the more noisy and bright color of oil pastel and gouache in *The Rooster Who Would Not Be Quiet!* The artist uses color to strike a quiet, almost somber, mood in *Town Is By the Sea*. In *The Rooster Who Would Not be Quiet!* notice the change to the use of blue and gray when the town of La Paz elects a mayor who insists on quiet with the noisy orange and yellow of the singing Gallito and the bustling town before and after the oppressive term of this mayor. The color black is used to strong effect in *Town by the Sea* to show the father's somber working conditions and with menacing effect in *The Journey* by Francesca Sanna. Red is also a strong color used in *The Journey* where even a small amount serves to draw the eye. In *Red*, by De Kinder, few other colors are used until the narrator breaks the silence surrounding bullying on the playground.

Line, shape, and perspective are other tools of the artist. Notice how the wavy black line of the seashore in *The Journey* changes to the shape of grasping and destructive hands as war begins. The hand motif recurs in this book with strong use of shape and perspective as the small family is directed by an angry and giant guard to go back. The shape of the mother with her children is rounded and protective, while eyes and hands in the dark are menacing and sharp. The playground bully in *Red* is depicted as a huge menacing shape with pointed teeth and grasping hands in one double-spread where the narrator is a small figure in the bottom right corner depicting her fear and feelings of helplessness.

Imagery may also be used symbolically in visual arts such as migrating birds in *The Journey* or the caged drum with wings in *Drum Dream Girl*. The kite shown in every image in *Malala/Iqbal* is an expression of freedom that visually connects her story with that of Iqbal. In *The Secret Project*, a Hopi Indian doll floats in the sky above the laboratory for the secret and destructive invention.

One further decision made in the illustration of a picture book is the use of framing. This is clear in *Sidewalk Flowers*. When someone is shown only in part in the frame, it gives a sense of immense size and power, for example, the pointing hand in *The Rooster Who Would Not Be Quiet!* when the mayor is fired. Framing may lead us to draw comparisons. In *The Journey*, the family of mother and two children surrounded by dark hands contrasts with a framed image of the same family including the father in happier times conveyed in part by the oval shape. The contrast of who is in each frame is striking and speaks volumes about the family's loss. Some illustrators are very stylized in their use of frames. Jeanette Winter's use of geometric shapes in *Malala/Iqbal* along with the vertical panels holds the images very still, providing small vignettes rather than continuing action. The round frames on several key pages in *Wolf in the Snow* serve to contrast the girl with the wolf; the dual circles are almost lens in a pair of glasses, but the broken, somewhat squiggly line around each is more dynamic than solid perfectly round circles. Color and framing are used powerfully in *The Secret Project* as most pages are framed in white until the test of the "gadget" when the frames become shades of gray eventually leading to an opening of solid black pages, with the author's note framed in black.

READING PICTURE BOOKS WITH A CRITICAL LITERACY LENS

Readers need to ask many of the same critical questions about picture books as with other literature, but in this case, a layer of complexity is added through the addition of the images. Now readers need to consider the messages conveyed not only in the text but also in the illustrations *and* in the juxtaposition of the images and text. Students in upper grades likely have some experience talking about inferences, point of view, and even bias in the written texts they read. But despite their early experiences with picture books, they may have very little to no experience talking about these features in visual or audiovisual media. We live in a very visual culture with Instagram, advertisement, the Internet, television, and other media and should not neglect teaching our students to think critically about themselves both as consumers and as producers of those images.

We can start our discussion with a wordless book such as *Sidewalk Flowers*. In this book, a young child in a red jacket accompanies an adult as they walk through an urban neighborhood. The child stops to pick flowers growing in small cracks and spaces in the urban landscape. Without words, we are left to make several assumptions that we might ask our students to unpack. First, what is the gender of the child? The flowery endpapers and the child's actions picking and then distributing the flowers might be taken as female. But why do we assume that? How is our reaction different if we think of the character as a young boy? Students might be asked to look for how flowers are used in advertisements. Is there an appeal to a particular gender? Does the advertiser seek to create a gentle mood, and why? We might also assume the adult is the child's father and that they are walking home where both are met by an embrace from the child's mother and man's wife. Viewers could be asked to talk about how the illustrator has positioned us to make these assumptions but also to look for ways our assumptions might be challenged. For example, who are the young children in the backyard, and how are they related to the other characters? While the child is noticing flowers, tattoos, a cat in the window, and a dead bird, the adult seems distracted with a cell phone. What is the message of this book about adults and children? How do we know the adult is still paying attention to the child? How is the sparing use of color used to tell the story? What do we notice about the neighborhoods the two walk through? What kinds of people do they pass, and who do they pay attention to? Both an author and an illustrator are attributed with this book. How do you think the author conveyed this story to the illustrator? What would you imagine the conversation might have been between the author and the illustrator? Who was most empowered to tell this story and in what ways?

Many of the picture books in this chapter deal with tough topics such as the depiction of slavery in *Freedom in Congo Square* as the days of the week countdown until Sundays when enslaved people are free to gather in the city square. Viewers could discuss how the harsh treatment is not shown explicitly, but the illustrator uses bent-over bodies and shows how nighttimes were spent in close and restrictive quarters. In *I Like, I Don't Like* images of children eating popcorn, playing soccer and talking on a cell phone are juxtaposed with images of child

---

Sidebar 12.1   Question Stems for Discussing Picture Books

- How are people and cultures represented in the images?
- What are the outstanding features of the images—the use of color or shape? The size or relative size of characters or objects in the image?
- What information is conveyed in the illustrations?
- How is the image framed, and what is not in the picture?
- What symbolism is present in the images?
- Where does the artist draw our attention? How?
- From whose point of view do we see the images?
- How is the viewer positioned relative to the image?
- What is the relationship of the illustrator to the topic/culture/setting portrayed?

labor to produce these products, and the contrast is underscored with a very simple text, "I like soccer balls" and "I don't like soccer balls." In *Malala/Iqbal*, both characters are the victims of violence. The illustrations and text work together to tell us their contrasting and connected stories. Their gaze positions the viewer as a witness and demonstrates their defiance and agency.

In a picture book, decisions are made about the placement of the text on the page. In *Freedom in Congo Square* the text is usually provided on straight lines, but on two full spreads it isn't; how does this convey the meaning of these pages? In *The Book Itch* words are incorporated in the images as they are depicted on the endpapers and signage. The use of different font sizes and weights in the text visually underscore important quotes. The "Kee-kee-ree-KEE" of the Gallito's song in *The Rooster Who Would Not Be Quiet!* spring from the pages and even fill one full spread in loud defiance of the decree "no singing."

When using picture books with older students, one might use a variety of strategies. Read the story without showing the pictures, and ask students how they envision the characters or the action. Then show the pictures, and have students discuss what was surprising and to what purpose. Alternatively, the teacher may take students through a picture walk of the book without sharing the words—or use a wordless book and have students narrate the story. A teacher might open a discussion by asking students to choose an image from the story and take turns sharing their choices. Instead of asking students to respond with spoken or written words, a teacher might ask students to create their own images as a response, perhaps using collage with magazine images. Picture books and visual arts provide a time to highlight the students in a classroom who are particularly talented visually.

In Chapter 13, we discuss the strategy of asynchronous discussion. An asynchronous discussion promotes reflection before constructing a response. In the case of a picture book, it allows students time to study the images as well as the texts before responding.

Sidebar 12.2   Awards for Picture Books

- Caldecott Medal http://www.ala.org/alsc/awardsgrants/bookmedia/caldecottmedal/caldecottmedal
- New York Times Best Illustrated Books for Children https://www.nytimes.com/2018/11/02/books/best-illustrated-childrens-books-2018.html
- Coretta Scott King Illustrator Award http://www.ala.org/rt/emiert/cskbookawards
- Pura Belpre Illustrator Award http://www.ala.org/alsc/awardsgrants/bookmedia/belpremedal
- Boston Globe/Hornbook Picture Book Award https://www.hbook.com/boston-globe-horn-book-awards/

ANNOTATED BIBLIOGRAPHY

Baccelliere, Anna. *I Like, I Don't Like*. 2017. 28 pp. Ale + Ale. Eerdman's Books for
Young Readers. 9780802854803
While every child may have the right to play, some of the subjects of that play, a
soccer ball, a car, or music, may represent child labor elsewhere. Each opening
spread features "I like," with children enjoying play, and "I don't like," with a child
doing work related to that play, often to support a family.

Cordell, Matthew. *Wolf in the Snow*. 2017. 48p. Feiwel and Friends. 9781250076366
A young girl lost in the snow helps a wolf pup reunite with the pack who in turn assist
the girl to return to her family. The snowy wordless book conveys the universal love
of family for the young.

Deedy, Carmen Agra. *The Rooster Who Would Not Be Quiet!* Yelchin, Eugene. 2017. 48 pp.
Scholastic Press. 9780545722889
A noisy village elects a mayor who promises peace and quiet, and fear drives everyone to silence until one day a noisy rooster appears. No effort by the mayor can
silence the rooster until one day he threatens to kill the noisy bird, but the people
rally to demonstrate the song will not be silenced. Brightly colored illustrations
accompany the lively parable of authoritarian rule and dissent.

De Kinder, Jan. *Red*. Translated by Laura Watkinson. 2015. 32 pp. Eerdman's Books for
Young Readers. 9780802854469
One day a classmate's taunt turns into bullying on the playground. Others are
afraid to speak up until one student raises her hand and empowers others to tell the
teacher what has happened.

Engle, Margarita. *Drum Dream Girl: How One Girl's Courage Changed Music*. López,
Rafael. 2015. 48 pp. Houghton Mifflin Harcourt. 9780544102293
A young girl dreams of playing the drums, but everyone including her father tells
her girls don't play drums. Vibrant, dreamy illustrations depict the tropical island
of Cuba and evoke the folk art of the island. Imagery of wings and one image of a
drum in a cage with wings underscore the dreamy mood of the story, while some
pages turn to be tall scenes of carnival and the caged drum.

Lawson, JonArno. *Sidewalk Flowers*. Smith, Sydney. 2015. 32 pp. Groundwood Books.
9781554984312
A young girl in a red hood accompanies her father walking home from the mar-
ket through a diverse neighborhood. While he is frequently distracted with a cell
phone call, she is noticing and sharing small flowers in the urban landscape.

Love, Jessica. *Julian Is a Mermaid*. 2018. 40 pp. Candlewick. 9780763690458
Julian is enchanted by the mermaids he encounters with his abuela on the subway,
and when they get home, he dresses up in a filmy curtain and headdress of fern
fronds. The outfit is complete when Abuela presents him with a strand of beads
and leads him to join a mermaid parade. Watercolor, gouache, and ink illustrations against a warm brown background complete the picture of imagination and
acceptance.

Nelson, Vaunda Micheaux. *The Book Itch: Freedom, Truth, & Harlem's Greatest Bookstore*. Gregory, Christie R. 2015. 32 pp. Lerner/Carolrhoda. 9780761339434
A young boy narrates the story of The National Memorial African Bookstore in
Harlem owned by his father. Images and fonts offer a tribute to the power of words
and truth.

Robertson, Robbie. *Hiawatha and the Peacemaker*. Shannon, David. 2015. 48 pp. Abrams. 9781419712203

The story of the Great Peacemaker, who suffered from a speech impediment, and his chosen speaker, Hiawatha, who traveled with him to spread a message of peace and unite the five nations of the Iroquois people. Thought to have lived in the fourteenth century in what is now North America, their method of representational government and law of peace are believed to have influenced Thomas Jefferson and other authors of the U.S. Constitution; a long story about creating peace and unity through nonviolence and forgiveness with brilliantly colored dramatic illustrations.

Sanat, Dan. *After the Fall: How Humpty Dumpty Got Back up Again*. 2017. 48 pp. Roaring Brook Press. 9781626726826

What happened to the infamous Humpty after he was put back together? Among other things a fear of heights. In this humorous telling we hear from Humpty, illustrations expand the story and provide the humor; an exercise in looking closely at images for clues and thinking about alternative stories to the ones we think we know.

Sanna, Francesca. *The Journey*. 2016. 48 pp. Flying Eye Books. 9781909263994

Forced to flee their homes by a war that has taken their father, two children and their mother embark on a dangerous journey across many borders in search of a new home. Striking illustrations depict the danger and hope of refugees.

Schwartz, Joanne. *Town Is by the Sea*. Smith, Sydney. 2017. 52 pp. Groundwood Books.

In text and striking ink and watercolor illustrations, the world of a young boy's bright day near the sea is contrasting with the dark world inhabited by his father, who is working in a mine under the sea.

Weatherford, Carole Boston. *Freedom in Congo Square*. Christie, R. Gregory. 2016. 40 pp. Little Bee Books. 9781499801033

A poem celebrates the end of six days of hard work when slaves and free people meet at Congo Square in New Orleans. Rhyming couplets count down the days filled with hard work, beatings, despair, and attempts to run away with Sundays protected by law. A foreword and an author's note provide historical context. Stylized illustrations show back-breaking work contrasting the jubilation and musical celebration of Sundays gathered in the square.

Wenzel, Brendan. *They All Saw a Cat*. 2016. 44 pp. Chronicle. 9781452150130

A child, a dog, a fish, a bee, a flea, and a bat all see the same cat, but for each it looks different; fun title for teaching point of view and representation. A very young child is depicted, and the text is simple and repetitive. The artwork is sophisticated and may provoke discussion about how we see others (and ourselves).

Winter, Jeanette. *Malala/Iqbal: Two Stories of Bravery*. 2014. 40 pp. Beach Lane Books. 9781481422949

Two activists are featured in complementary stories: you must close and rotate the book to read the second. Malala is well known for her fight for the education of girls, while Iqbal's story fighting child labor is less well known and ends tragically. A double-spread with the symbolic kite ties the two together in the middle opening.

Winter, Jonah. *The Secret Project*. Winter, Jeanette. 2017. 40 pp. Beach Lane Books. 9781481469135

In a remote desert location, scientists gather for a secret project: the creation and testing of the first atomic bomb. Somber colors and a quiet text present the story in a picture book format. An author's note provides the historical context and the devastating deployment of the weapon in Hiroshima and Nagasaki.

13

Using Asynchronous Discussion to Unpack Visual Messages (Lesson Plan)

An asynchronous discussion contrasts with a real-time discussion because participants are not all engaged in the conversation at the same time. Instead, they have time to review and think about the prompt or classmate responses before constructing their own. The process lends itself to a reflective construction of responses. In large classrooms, the class period may be over before all students have the chance to participate in a real-time discussion. An asynchronous discussion allows everyone a voice in the conversation. An asynchronous discussion thus disrupts the typical classroom discussion where the teacher asks a question and students must wait to be called on before they answer. Quieter students have the same opportunity to participate as their more extroverted classmates. Grisham and Wolsey (2006) suggest a threaded discussion as a way to "recenter" the focus of student learning with the advantage of being both interactive like oral discussion and thoughtful like written communication.

Asynchronous discussions are most often associated with online learning spaces such as Blackboard or other classroom management systems that include a threaded discussion feature that allows students to post responses to one another in addition to their original response to a teacher prompt. Edmodo and other programs also exist where K-12 teachers can set up online discussions. The use of technology is appealing and natural to students. In many classrooms students have access to individual devices. Larson (2009) found this allowed students to move seamlessly from reading to responding; they did not have to wait a turn or rush to keep up with classmates before engaging in a discussion. Grisham and Wolsey (2006) compared online responses in literature circles to written journal responses and found students thought more deeply for the asynchronous discussion where they perceived their audience was a group of peers and not just the teacher.

Prompts may include a passage, an image, or other multimedia for students to respond to. Larson (2009) details what happened when fifth-grade students asked to be able to create their own prompts. Student-created prompts led to a meaningful learning experience of how to develop a good prompt and also gave students ownership of the discussion. Another asynchronous model features a moderated blog where students to respond to a teacher prompt using the comments feature. The teacher can review student comments before they are made public. A shared Google Doc or Wiki may also allow students to "chat" asynchronously or to build a document together. Protocols such as using the @studentname to indicate the response is to a particular classmate should be developed. In a large class, asynchronous discussions can become unwieldy if students are asked to respond to everyone else in the class—assigning students to small groups allows for more depth in the discussion.

There are ways to conduct an asynchronous discussion that are not online. Bintz and Shelton (2004) describe using a strategy of "written conversation" where pairs of students share a notebook and pencil. As the teacher stops at key points in a book, students are instructed to silently talk to each other by taking turns writing in the notebook. This strategy could easily be adopted in a classroom with a picture book read aloud. Other examples might involve using a cooperative learning strategy of "Graffiti" where students write responses to a prompt on chart paper or on sticky notes that are added to the chart. Students can then be encouraged to read what others have written and post their own responses. Another strategy involves giving students so many colored dots and asking them to review what others have written and "vote" with their dots on issues they want to continue to discuss. The leader of the discussion can then see the burning topics and lead a further discussion of select responses. Students might write individual responses and place in an envelope that is then passed to another group who open the envelope and share out responses, threading the discussion with additional responses. The envelope could be passed until they come to original groups who open and read all responses to their "posts" and summarize to share out.

In an eighth-grade classroom such as Maria's, students have experience using social media and enjoy chatting online. They are also capable of leading their own discussions. Maria has spent considerable time talking with students about what makes a good prompt. Students have been placed in small groups of four. Each group has been assigned a different spread (two-page opening) from the book *The Journey* and provided a Google Doc for its discussion. All students have been assigned a color font that is also associated with their role in the discussion. Green is for go; this role is responsible for asking the original question and for posing new questions in the discussion. Red is for hot; this role is meant to be provocative by posing strong opinions. Blue is cool; this role should be a more neutral observer referring to either the image or the remarks of others. Orange is caution; this role should question conclusions or provide statements such as "I wonder. . . ." An alternative use of the color coding would be to ask every student to provide at least one response in each color.

An asynchronous discussion allows for more thoughtful, reflective participation, and students may need time to process their responses from within their role. For this reason a teacher may want to have this activity open over several class periods directing students to check in with their group's Google Doc at different times or as homework outside of class with clear expectations that students will read and respond at least four to five times each. In the scenario in Chapter 12, Maria has asked the school librarian, Philip, to introduce and read aloud the book *The Journey* to her students. As the asynchronous discussion will occur in the background of her class for several days, Philip has also offered to help moderate student work. In addition, his expertise with Google Docs has been helpful in setting up the lesson.

The following is an opening lesson for a unit on immigration and refugees. The asynchronous quality allows it to occur in the background over several days perhaps while the teacher is assessing a previous unit or providing other instructional activities related to the topic. Philip has also recommended a related unit from PBS, *The Global Refugee Crisis: A Community Responds*, available at http://www.pbs.org/pov/4point1miles/lesson-plan/, which would be an appropriate companion to this lesson. This activity assumes students have ready access to a device, the Internet, and Google documents, but it could also be done with chart paper and different color markers if online access is not available.

Several critical literacy elements may be addressed in this lesson. The most salient element is attention to the social and political issues addressed in texts (Lewison, Flint, & Van Sluys, 2002). "Texts" in this case refers to the images that provide striking commentary about refugees and the dangers they face as well as their hopes for freedom. The author/illustrator has a clearly sympathetic perspective that may counter some portrayals of immigrants in the media. The picture book medium allows readers to go beyond the surface to consider the messages conveyed through artistic elements such as line, shape, color, and framing in the construction of images. Viewers are asked to consider how images like other texts are laden with social and political ideas and ideologies and can begin to extend this understanding to other visual messages in advertising and politics. Images also ask us to "talk back" rather than passively accepting their ideological and social perspectives.

Table 13.1   Lesson Plan

Central focus: Students will *analyze* how visual images utilize line, shape, color, and other artistic techniques to convey social and political messages.	**Subjects:** Social studies and English language arts
Grade: 8	**Classroom context:** Whole class to small groups; lesson collaboratively planned with the librarian
Standards	

Standards

CCSS.ELA-Literacy.SL.8.2
Analyze the purpose of information presented in diverse media and formats (e.g., visually, quantitatively, orally) and evaluate the motives (e.g., social, commercial, political) behind its presentation.
CCSS.ELA-Literacy.SL.8.1.b
Follow rules for collegial discussions and decision-making, track progress toward specific goals and deadlines, and define individual roles as needed.

(Continued)

Table 13.1   Lesson Plan (Continued)

Objectives

Students will *know* how to analyze visual elements including the use of line, color, shape, and framing to convey information and values.

Students will *understand* that visual images carry social and political messages and values.

Students will *be able to* create responses to a text following a protocol with an assigned role in discussion.

Assessment: During the introductory lesson in the library, the teacher librarian will assess that all students are able to locate the Google Doc with their group assignment. The teacher librarian will also monitor engagement with the whole class discussion about the cover image and student understanding of the assignment. Individual assessment of participation in the Google conversation can be accomplished by examining the assigned color for each student. The teacher librarian plans to log in with each group at least daily to assess participation and intervene if a group is stuck or otherwise off track. Google Docs also allows the teachers to monitor the history to see when students are editing the document. Students will be evaluated on frequent, thoughtful, and complete responses and their performance within the assigned role using a rubric (Figure 13.2). Students can be asked to use the same rubric for a self-assessment following the activity. Finally, each student will be asked to write a paragraph about the page the student was assigned to discuss using at least three of the artistic techniques discussed: use of color, line, shape, size, frame, and symbolism.

Materials: Copy of the book *The Journey*. Document projector. Student devices (one per student is preferred) with access to Google Docs. Google Docs should be set up ahead of time for small groups to share; students can be invited to their assigned group document through e-mail. Multiple copies of the book will facilitate students' exploration of their assigned page, but a copy is not essential for every student. This book can also be found online in the following lesson plan: https://www.amnesty.org .uk/files/exploring_the_journey_together.pdf
The video *The Global Refugee Crisis: A Community Responds* http://www.pbs.org/pov/4point1miles/lesson-plan/ is also recommended with this lesson.

Academic language function: Analyze	**Language demands:** Listening to a teacher read aloud and attending to the visual images as well as the words; creating written responses to a prompt and to peers

Lesson introduction

1. The librarian projects the cover of the book, *The Journey*, by Francesca Sanna on a large screen and asks students what they think the book is about.

2. The librarian asks, "As you look at this cover and think about the title, *The Journey*, what do you think this book is about? What clues do you find in the images to support your ideas about the topic? What mood or emotion do you think the cover suggests? Why?" The students are given time to discuss their ideas.

3. The librarian says, "An artist uses line, shape, color, and frame to tell a story or convey an idea or mood. What do you notice about the use of color in this image?" Students are prompted to talk about the use of black and red in the image. The librarian asks, "Are there particular shapes in this image that grab your attention?" Students may respond about the large hand, the relative size and rounded shapes of the people, and the mountain shape of the overall image. The librarian points out the images of birds on the cover and asks about the possible symbolism related to the title. For example, birds migrate or birds represent flight or freedom.

4. The librarian says, "Now I am going to read straight through the book while you listen and view the illustrations. Let's save comments and questions for later; I want you to get the overall story from the text and illustrations." The librarian places the book under a document camera and reads aloud straight through the book, *The Journey*, with the images projected so that students can follow along.

5. The librarian leads the class in a small discussion about their predictions and what the story was about by returning to the cover image and pointing out aspects that were part of the class observations and predictions about the book. "Were we correct in our prediction about the meaning of the title? What type of journey was portrayed in this book?" The librarian underscores the importance of the images in conveying the story. "As you look at this cover image now, what do you notice that was important in the book?" Students should note the hand, the use of black, the suitcases, the people, and the birds.

6. The librarian asks "Now that I have closed the book, what pages or images do you remember most?" and elicits multiple responses.

7. The librarian states, "You will have an opportunity to examine one of these pages in detail to think about how the artist conveyed these strong and memorable messages."

Instructional input

8. The librarian tells students, "In the next week you will be assigned to work in a small group to examine an opening (two pages) in the book to talk about how the illustrator used line, color, shape, framing, and other techniques to convey the story."

9. The librarian tells each student they should open their device and log in to e-mail to find an invitation to the Google Doc where they will be working. The Google Doc will be set up to show their assigned two-page opening from the book, their group members, and their role in the discussion.

10. The librarian models the roles of Green, Red, Blue, and Orange (Figure 13.1) and sample stems for each role on a projector showing how to change the font color and using the book cover. The librarian says, "The person in the Green role has the important job of starting the discussion. I might ask about the

(Continued)

Table 13.1   Lesson Plan (Continued)

cover, 'What information or emotion is conveyed by the artist through color in this image?'" The librarian shows how to change the font color to green and write the question. "The person in the Red role is expected to share a strong opinion, 'Clearly the use of the color black is ominous and threatening in the hands and the shadowy figure at the top but it also draws our attention to the family members who have black hair.' Blue is a neutral role and this person should make observations or state clear facts. For example, she might say, 'There is a lot of blue and green on the cover,' and Red might respond, 'I think that has a calming effect.' The job of Orange is to slow down the discussion and provoke deeper reflection, 'Why do you think the illustrator used so much blue and green on the cover?'" With each role, the librarian models how to change the font color and type in the response on a new line. The librarian emphasizes that students do not need to take turns in any particular order once Green has posted the first question. The librarian asks for student suggestions for each role to check for understanding.

11. The librarian reviews what is meant by "asynchronous discussion." "Over the next several days you will be engaging in an asynchronous discussion. 'Asynchronous' means not happening at the same time. The opposite of 'asynchronous' is 'synchronous.' Have you ever seen the synchronous swimming competition in the Olympics? Everyone is making the same move at the same time. We have been engaged in a synchronous discussion because we are all in the room together at the same time. In an asynchronous discussion you do not need to be in the Google document at the same time. In fact, it might be good to log in to the document, read what has been written, and then take some time to think about what to say next and how to say it from your assigned role. And then return to the document to post your next response."

12. The librarian reminds students about having a discussion, "I know you have learned from your teacher what makes a good discussion, and the assigned roles are also meant to lead you to ask questions, state opinions, and respond thoughtfully to each other. Remember when you log in to use your assigned font color to respond."

13. "The discussion may begin to branch in different directions so you can insert responses anywhere in the document. In the example I shared, Orange might also decide to respond to Red's comment about the use of black, asking, 'Would the effect have been different if the hands were red?'" The librarian demonstrates how to insert a response using the orange font.

14. The librarian reminds students that they will be returning to the classroom where their teacher will share expectations about when they should log in to their group's asynchronous discussion. "I look forward to reading what you post as I will be checking in with each group daily." The librarian sends several copies of the book back to the classroom with the teacher.

Work session

15. The classroom teacher needs to think about how best to facilitate an asynchronous discussion in a synchronous class. She may want to give each color a time during the class period to log in to their group's Google Doc, while the rest of the class is engaged in other activities starting with Green who needs to create the opening question.

16. Simultaneous with this asynchronous discussion, the teacher might introduce a unit on immigration and refugees. The PBS *The Global Refugee Crisis: A Community Responds*, http://www.pbs.org/pov/4point1miles/lesson-plan/, offers several ideas. Alternatively, the asynchronous discussion of *The Journey* might occur the week before the unit opens as a preview.

17. The discussion will likely remain open over several days to allow everyone a chance to participate and reflect between responses. Students will need access to their group's image; there need to be at least enough copies of the book for each group. This book can also be found online in the following lesson plan:

    https://www.amnesty.org.uk/files/exploring_the_journey_together.pdf

18. The teacher should set some minimal expectation for participation, such as an additional three to five responses, beyond the initial response.

19. Once the discussion period is closed, students should be asked to review their group's discussion and write a paragraph about the overall message in their assigned image using at least three of the vocabulary of line, shape, color, size, frame, and symbolism.

20. Students should also complete a self-assessment of their role in the discussion using the rubric.

Lesson closure

21. The teacher reads *The Journey* aloud again pausing for each of the assigned spreads to allow discussion of the visual elements and message on each page. The teacher asks for each assigned spread, "First let's hear from the group assigned to this page. What were some of the things you want us to notice about the art work?" Then the teacher opens the discussion, "For those of you who were not in this group, what else do you notice? Are there any connections with the page you discussed? Do you have any questions for the group assigned to this page?"

22. Finally, the teacher makes connections to the unit on immigration and refugees.

Differentiation: Roles and/or groups may be assigned based on the ability to create heterogeneous groups. The teacher may modify the writing requirements based on students' levels of readiness. The teacher may also assign page spreads to groups based on interest in particular topics related to the book.

Green is for GO!
Writes the original prompt/asks new questions

- What do you see. . .?
- How did the artist. . .?
- What is the tone or emotion. . .?

Red is Hot!
Expresses strong opinions

- I believe. . . .
- I think. . . .
- It's obvious. . . .

Blue is Neutral
Makes observations without opinion

- I observe. . . .
- I see. . . .
- There are. . . .

Orange is Cautious
Slows down the discussion to consider other possibilities

- I'm not sure about. . . .
- I wonder. . . .
- Have you thought about. . .?

Figure 13.1   Roles for Asynchronous Discussion

From *Genre-Based Strategies to Promote Critical Literacy in Grades 4–8* by Danielle E. Hartsfield and Sue C. Kimmel. Santa Barbara, CA: Libraries Unlimited. Copyright © 2020.

Asynchronous Group Discussion Rubric

Name _____

Role _____

	Excellent	Good	Acceptable	Unacceptable
Frequency	Posts at least four times in addition to original post, and posts are distributed throughout the discussion period.	Posts at least three times in addition to the original post.	Posts at least three times, but most posts are completed early or late in the discussion.	Fewer than three posts.
Initial post	Initial post is well developed within assigned role.	Initial post is within assigned role but lacks complete development.	Initial post lacks complete development and is too generic for assigned role.	Initial post is missing, poorly developed, or too short to add substance.
Follow-up posts	Follow-up posts are timely, build on the responses of others, and raise further questions.	Follow-up posts build on the responses of others.	Follow-up posts address the responses of others.	Follow-up posts are missing or fail to connect with other posts.
Role	Student remains within the assigned role and effectively performs the role to extend thoughtful discussion.	Student remains within the assigned role to add to the discussion.	Student mostly remains within the assigned role.	Student fails to perform the assigned role.
Clarity and mechanics	Writing is clear, concise, and free of grammatical or typographical errors.	Writing is clear and mostly free of grammatical or typographical errors.	Writing is mostly clear, and a few grammatical or typographical errors do not detract from the meaning.	Writing lacks clarity, is too long or short, or contains errors that prevent effective communication.

Figure 13.2   Rubric for Asynchronous Group Discussion

MODIFYING THE LESSON PLAN

An asynchronous discussion allows time for reflection between responses, encourages full participation, and can occur across multiple days. If students have access to the technology outside of the class period, much of the activity might be completed as homework, particularly since the pages of *The Journey* can also be accessed online. While this lesson was designed for a classroom familiar with working in a context where technology is accessible, it can be adapted for use in classrooms that do not have ubiquitous access to devices and Google documents. Students might be provided with colored markers or colored sticky notes and encouraged to post and read responses on chart paper or in a shared journal that is passed along. A teacher or school librarian could design the lesson to take place in a class period or over several days where time is allotted to the activity or small groups rotate through. For example, Green students might be given ten minutes early in a class period, while other students work on another project. Younger students would require more scaffolding to construct meaningful discussion posts with significant modeling from the teacher, sentence stems to complete, and teacher-provided prompts for discussion. Colors could be assigned to other roles, for example, those of a literature circle similar to the one described in Chapter 9.

Picture books are accessible to all ages, and the vocabulary of color, size, and shape can be introduced to very young children and used in critical literacy discussions of the images in a picture book. School librarians and teachers could add this vocabulary to their sharing of picture books with students.

In this scenario, the school librarian was a key partner in the application of technology to the activity and for his expertise in literature including picture books. The inclusion of a second educator also facilitates the back-channel aspect of this activity where students may be completing the activity outside of regular classroom time and supervision. Given the involvement of the librarian in introducing and monitoring the discussion, he should also assess student work in this area.

14

Graphic Novels

In Jamie's class, students have been reading the Eisner Award–winning graphic novel Ghosts *by Raina Telgemeier. Jamie is amazed at how her students have taken to the format; different students have emerged as expert readers in this format, and students have grasped vocabulary and applied skills of inference she would otherwise have to drag them through. She did share what she was doing ahead of time with the principal, who suggested she send a letter home to parents since there continues to be misunderstanding about the intellectual effort needed to read what some would dismiss as just a comic book. The school librarian offered her some references about the value of graphic novels to include in the letter.*

Today her students are working with a partner to examine a single page in a graphic novel they are reading as a class book. Partners have been asked to list out everything they have learned from this page about the characters, setting, plot, and mood indicating the evidence. They are prompted to think about the cultural and social implications from the images and text on the page, including identifying race, gender, and ethnicity, if possible, as well as social class, religion, or other features they might be able to infer. In addition, they are asked to look at the power relations on the page—how are relative size, use of perspective, framing, and so on used? Jamie asks students to consider whose point of view is privileged on the page through these elements.

Students are engaged in lively discussion and debate as they bring their own backgrounds and experiences to the assignment. One student can be heard asking his partner about how Día de los Muertos is depicted on the page they have chosen to talk about. Following a conversation she had with the school librarian, Jamie has been waiting for someone to raise this question. The two were talking at lunch one day about her plans to use the book with students, and the librarian shared some of the controversy she had discovered through one of the blogs she follows. They have planned a lesson together to encourage students to reframe the inclusion of the religious observance in the graphic novel. Chapter 15, the final chapter of this text, gives educators guidance about how they can develop a lesson like Jamie's.

DEFINING GRAPHIC NOVELS

Graphic novels are a comic book format where the action moves sequentially through frames that include visual images and words. They are generally distinguished from comic books by their length and binding. Comic books are often on magazine-quality paper and stapled in the middle, while graphic novels usually have paperback quality or even a hardcover binding. The term "graphic novel" has stuck despite the fact that many graphic novels feature nonfiction texts. The term "novel" is seen rather as an indication of the novel length of the text. Graphic novels have been recognized for their multimodal format supporting a variety of visual and textual literacies.

Given their relationship and similarity to comic books along with their popularity with kids, adults, including teachers and librarians, frequently (still) question their validity as literature. Some suggest "at least the kids are reading," or these serve best as a gateway to "real" reading. Clark (2014) found preservice social studies teachers were reluctant to use graphic novels in their future classrooms, feeling professionally constrained by their fear of pushback from community and school members. Connors (2012) reported similar attitudes among preservice teachers. In their report of an action research project using graphic novels and conducted by the school librarian, Bosma, Rule, and Krueger (2013) described a setting where teachers were skeptical and reluctant to use graphic novels for instruction.

Bosma et al. (2013) found students achieved similar or better recall of complex historical events when these were introduced in a graphic novel compared with reading prose with illustrations. In addition, students reported enjoying the format much more. In fact, the ability to "read" both pictures and text and to understand how to move through and make meaning from the frames on the page involves complex reading skills. Jiménez and Meyer (2016) conducted think-aloud studies with expert readers of graphic novels and uncovered a complex visual, spatial, and textual process requiring the reader to synthesize the three to comprehend the graphic format. Graphic novels appear to be a relatively quick read for a classroom text; however, as depicted in the scenario opening this chapter, these authors suggest each page is worthy of in-depth discussion and examination. The pages of a graphic novel are layered with complexity, and students should be encouraged to slow down to attend to information in both the text and the images.

There's some blurring of lines between comic books and graphic novels. For example, Marvel's *Ms. Marvel* is comic book length but has appeared on numerous graphic novel lists. This story about a Muslim teen girl from Jersey City breaks boundaries of gender, culture, and religion in the choice of heroine. Cultures clash early in this series as Zoe, a White teenager, "blonde and popular" makes insensitive comments about Nakia's headscarf. The main character, sixteen-year-old Kamala who writes Avengers fan fiction, deals with a devout Muslim brother and a protective father. She sneaks out to join a teenage party and transforms into a blonde superheroine to rescue a drowning Zoe. The emergence of her superpowers and alternate identity raises questions about her ethnic and religious identity. As she embraces her mission to defend the greater good and protect those who can't defend themselves, she chooses a costume reflective of her cultural identity.

Readers and fans of superhero movies and comics will be attracted to this book that also allows exploration of Muslim culture and struggles of bicultural teens. Numerous picture books and book choices for new readers also employ many of the features of graphic novels, such as speech bubbles and panels. Several of the picture books discussed in Chapter 12 such as *Wolf in the Snow* and *Sidewalk Flowers*, for example, use these features.

EVALUATING GRAPHIC NOVELS

Graphic novels should be dynamic as there are both the interaction of images and text and the use of frames to create action on the page. As with other forms of storytelling, a graphic novel should be evaluated on how clearly the story is conveyed and organized with a beginning, middle, and end, but in the case of a graphic novel, the sequencing of the visual as well as the text is important. A graphic novelist has the element of color; for example, pages may be muted or framed in a different color to signal a passage in a different time, place, or reality. The graphic novel, however, should be evaluated based on how the elements of image, speech bubbles, and frames move that story forward, develop characters, and convey emotion. The graphic novelist has multiple elements to use for this purpose, and the evaluation should consider how well these work together. Thought bubbles as well as speech bubbles and other structural elements are available to the graphic novelist. Fans of graphic novels may feel they have access to a secret language of graphic novel tropes, some borrowed, for example, from manga such as hearts for eyes or cat ears.

A graphic novelist also applies the tools of picture book artists, including use of color, line, and movement through the pages. Gall and Gall (2015) suggest similar evaluative criteria can be applied to both. While picture books have wide open space to work in, the graphic novel uses smaller panels; a page may feature multiple images, so there is an ability to convey action. Gall and Gall (2015) provide several examples of where picture books and beginning readers also use panels and speech bubbles. The style of art used should match the story or have a good reason to juxtapose what is being said with what we see. Much of the criteria for evaluating picture books that was presented in Chapter 11 could be employed in the evaluation of visual images in graphic novels. Connors (2011) walks readers through an analysis of a graphic novel applying tools for looking at shape, perspective, and left–right visual structure in the images.

Like picture books, graphic novels lend themselves to critique of who is and is not included in the images that might feature a multicultural neighborhood or classroom, for example. The inclusion of disability (Moeller & Irwin, 2012) and different races (Moeller & Becnel, 2018) as well as stereotypes should also be considered. Graphic novels may be subject to challenge because they are "graphic," and the inclusion of images provides younger readers with potential access to nudity or graphic violence. Many comic books have been criticized for their inclusion of women (and men) dressed in revealing clothing. Parents and students may need to understand that many graphic novels are written for more mature audiences or reflect different cultural norms related to nudity or sexuality. As with any literature, we recommend that teachers preview the content before introducing in a classroom.

READING GRAPHIC NOVELS WITH A CRITICAL LITERACY LENS

Closely related to comic books where unlikely everyday people, such as Ms. Marvel, yield superpowers to fight injustice, the content of many graphic novels lends itself to themes of social justice. For example, in *The Shadow Hero*, Yang reintroduces readers to the Green Turtle, an Asian American superhero popular in the 1940s. Yang has created an origin story for the Green Turtle as the son of a grocer in Chinatown whose ambitious mother sees an opportunity for her son to become a superhero when she sews a costume for him. With training, he does gain strength, but when his father is killed by members of a tong, an organized crime group, he discovers a spirit that protected his father and now offers him a promise that he will never be shot. With that protection, he becomes the Jade Tortoise avenging his father. The afterword provokes discussion as well where Yang talks about the original Green Turtle, created by an early Asian American comic book author, Chu Hing. Hing wanted his character to be Chinese but was told no by his publisher. Yang shows us how we never see the face of the Green Turtle and other subtle ways Hing hid the cultural identity of his superhero.

Unusual choices for the hero or heroine often disrupt the ordinary in graphic novels. For example, an eleven-year-old Orthodox Jewish girl, Mirka, is featured in a series of graphic novels. In *Hereville: How Mirka Caught a Fish*, Mirka babysits her half sister, and they deal with a magical fish that carries a grudge. Deutsch's framing and use of color, speech bubbles, perspective, and other conventions of the graphic novel are strong compositions conveying character and plot. More unusual superheroes are featured in the <u>Lowriders in Space</u> series featuring a mosquito, an octopus, and a lowrider driving, female protagonist, Lupe the Impala. The trio journey to outer space and the center of Earth. Some science, Spanish language, Aztec culture, and lots of humor are included in the fun mix and adventurous stories. Latino culture is also featured in a collection of three Latin American folktales in *The Dragon Slayer*, which features several strong and clever female characters. Given that folklore and myths often feature characters with superpowers and the graphic novel's connection with superheroes, it's appropriate for the two to merge. George O'Connor has recast numerous Greek myths in graphic format, including the recent *Artemis*, a strong female protagonist who was goddess of the hunt and protector of women.

The concept of a superpower is given new meaning in *El Deafo* featuring Cece, a deaf protagonist. Wearing a phonic ear, a large device strapped to her chest, Cece realizes the device gives her superpowers, and she names herself "El Deafo," imagines herself dressed in a cape, and seeks a willing sidekick for her adventures. The memoir allows readers to inhabit the world of a deaf child struggling to read lips, understand words that are shouted, and navigate friendships as Cece worries about how others perceive her disability. The graphic novel disrupts our thinking about everyday abilities we may take for granted and provokes us to consider the superpowers developed by the hearing impaired to adapt to the hearing world. The characters in *El Deafo* are all depicted as rabbits with tall ears, exaggerating this feature in a book about the ability to hear. The graphic format of *El Deafo* requires the reader to study facial expressions and other clues much as a deaf person might use these clues to make sense of a communication.

In terms of challenging the commonplace and representing diversity, the elderly are rarely treated in books for children. *Sunny Side Up* uses imagery and text to give readers a view of a retirement community in Florida and its residents as Sunny spends an unexpected summer with her grandfather. There are numerous intertextual references to comics in this book that lead readers to think about invisibility and transformations in society. When Sunny makes a friend with Buzz, the groundskeeper's son, they discuss why even superheroes can't save the ones they love, a poignant message in this story of a family dealing with addiction. In one conversation about what superpower they would want, Sunny answers "invisibility," provoking possible discussion about what she means and what kinds of invisibility we see in society. When Sunny, her grandfather, and two women from the retirement home visit a cafeteria with an early bird special, the ladies tell Sunny to put a roll in her purse "in case you get hungry later." This scene, for example, might provoke a conversation about unseen kinds of poverty and food insecurity. Buzz's father, the groundskeeper, is a chemist from Cuba tending the grounds at a retirement home. As an aside, we learn that this former chemist learned to read English from comic books. At one point in the story, Sunny draws a connection between the comic book character Hulk who transforms into a giant monster when angered and her brother's behavior when on drugs. These references to other multimodal texts add layers of meaning to the book's themes related to aging, addiction, and family relationships.

Several graphic novels introduce cultural diversity and themes of social empowerment. *Pashmina* features an Indian American teenager, Pri, who is insulted with the name "Thrift Store" at school. Different expectations for females and family relationships in Indian culture are introduced as Pri travels to India to visit an aunt where she encounters poverty and a society where the status of women is subject to their husband's control. Before the trip, a magical shawl has transported Pri to an idealized India, but the magic doesn't work in India. As she and her aunt travel to discover the shawl's origin in India, she learns of an uprising of female workers and the intervention of the goddess Shakti. The shawl's magic was intended to allow women to see their choices and be empowered. Pri learns from her aunt the story of how her mother—young, unmarried, and pregnant—was forced to leave the country or bring disgrace to her family.

Understandings of social norms and culture are treated in several graphic novels set in schools. *Real Friends* addresses what it's like to be peripheral to the in-group, especially when your best friend is included and you are not. The images in this graphic novel often capture the social order within the group of girls and the feelings of being left out, for example, when Shannon is depicted as the court jester among royalty when she is with the in-group from school. In *Brave*, the character of Jensen is teased and bullied because of his weight and must navigate a confusing and often dangerous school culture. He describes getting through the school day "without getting eaten by the game monsters" in order to achieve a prize at the end of the level. The game motif, along with his fantasies of becoming a NASA astronaut and of acceptance at school, is visually depicted in bubble frames. *Brave* deals directly with transforming a culture that allows bullying as students in the story begin to address the ways culture might be changed one brick at a time.

Nonfiction is also featured in graphic novel format; a notable example is the acclaimed three-part <u>March</u> series by congressman John Lewis. Several authors have discussed the use of graphic novels in social studies classrooms, including addressing historical agency and positionality (Clark & Camicia, 2014). As Carano and Clabough (2016) suggest, a difficult concept such as civil disobedience may be more tangible when illustrated through a series of panels in a graphic novel, especially for less-experienced readers or English-language learners. In *March: Book One*, the first volume of the three-part memoir of John Lewis, readers are introduced to a comic book about Martin Luther King Jr. that circulated in the 1960s during the Civil Rights Movement.

Manga is a particular type of graphic novel from Japan that is wildly popular among many youth. The experience of reading a true manga is a cultural experience in itself as the book opens from what Westerners think of as the back of the book and is read from right to left. Instructions for how to read manga are often included in the book, but you can also find online videos (often produced by teens) explaining the format. In addition to the different ways the books are physically laid out and read, cultural tropes are used in manga; readers learn to recognize and "read" the way eyes are portrayed or different bubbles are used. Readers who struggle, in general, with reading graphic novels may be truly perplexed by manga. This sense of disorientation as one works to create meaning from the manga format allow readers a firsthand understanding of how literacy is cultural. The struggle "good" readers feel with manga may be similar to the struggles of readers in our classrooms with texts we take for granted. Graphic novels, in general, with their multimodal texts challenge readers to uncover levels of meaning in unfamiliar texts.

Low and Jacobs (2018) discuss new literature circle roles for graphic novels, including the "gutter dweller" who is responsible for considering the shape, size, and placement of panels and their meanings and "super fan" responsible

---

Sidebar 14.1   Question Stems for Graphic Novels

- How are frames and panels used to position the reader?
- Whose perspective is featured in the image? In the text?
- How is color used to convey theme or mood?
- How does the shape or size of a speech bubble add to the meaning of the text?
- In what ways is body language, gesture, or facial expressions important?

for connecting the graphic novel to other texts. Sun (2017) shares a study using graphic novels in a middle school classroom to promote critical literacy and shares the finding that the combination of text and visuals offered a multilayered experience for students to experience empathy, make connections to current events, and consider multiple perspectives. Smith and Pole (2018) discuss strategies for helping students to understand and "read" graphic novels paying attention to the use of color, gutters, panels, and other features and slowing down to pay attention to the visual information. Teachers cannot take for granted that students know how to attend to these features of graphic novels and need to spend time discussing the elements of graphic novels and how they work together to convey information about characters as well as cultural, social, and historical messages.

A familiar trope in both comic books and graphic novels is the unlikely hero or heroine who is reframed to possess the necessary superpower to right a wrong or fight evil. Everyone has the potential to take significant action to address social injustices. In the lesson in Chapter 15, students are provided the agency to investigate and reframe an issue of cultural appropriation in a positive and constructive manner.

ANNOTATED BIBLIOGRAPHY

Bell, Cece. *El Deafo*. 2014. 248 pp. Abrams. 9781419710209
     Young Cece is deaf and must wear a large hearing aid at school. These differences set her apart from her classmates, and she experiences a variety of responses from peers, including an eventual realization of the special powers of her superhearing aid.
Camper, Cathy. *Lowriders to the Center of the Earth*. Raul the Third. 2016. 128 pp. Chronicle Books. 9781452123431
     An unusual cast of characters including an octopus and a mosquito join Lupe the Impala on a journey to the underworld to retrieve their cat in a fast-paced adventure with numerous Spanish terms, folkloric references, and science concepts sprinkled throughout.
Chanani, Nidhi. *Pashmina*. 2017. 176 pp. First Second. 9781626720886
     Pri, an Indian American teenager, wonders about her mother's past and her own roots in India. She discovers a pashmina shawl that transports her to an idealized India, and when she travels to India, she learns more about the pashmina, her mother, family, and India.

Chmakova, Svetlana. *Brave*. 2017. 238 pp. Yen Press. 9780316363174
Navigating middle school is fraught with challenges for Jensen, who is slightly overweight and the target of bullying. His experiences shine a light on bullying within the school and for readers.

Deutsch, Barry. *Hereville: How Mirka Caught a Fish*. 2015. 146 pp. Abrams. 9781419708008
Mirka, a Jewish Orthodox girl, is the subject of several adventures. In this one, she is responsible for her younger sister when they tangle with a revengeful fish, and Mirka must exercise her unusual powers to save her family.

Hale, Shannon. *Real Friends*. Pham, LeUyen. 2017. 224 pp. First Second. 9781626724167
In this autobiographical story, young Shannon deals with issues of popularity, friendship, and growing up.

Hernandez, Jaime. *The Dragon Slayer: Folktales from Latin America*. Campoy, F. Isabel. 2018. 40 pp. Toon Graphics. 9781943145287
Three folktales from Latin America feature strong female protagonists.

Holm, Jennifer. *Sunny Side Up*. Holm, Matthew. 2015. 224 pp. Graphix. 9780545741651
Sunny's visit with her grandfather who lives in a retirement community in Florida is not the experience she expected. She meets her grandfather's friends and makes a friend herself. Humor abounds beside issues of aging, addiction, and family.

Jamieson, Victoria. *Roller Girl*. 2015. 240 pp. Dial Books for Young Readers. 9780525429678
Twelve-year-old Astrid joins a summer roller derby camp, and despite some hard falls, she perseveres and becomes a stronger player. The story deals with navigating friendships and parental expectations while featuring girls, sports, and positive mentoring by older players.

Lewis, John, & Andrew Aydin. *March: Book One*. Powell, Nate. 2013. 128 pp. Top Shelf Productions. 9781603093835
March: Book Two. 2015. 9780606365475
March: Book Three. 2016. 9781603094023
Key events from the Civil Rights Movement are featured in this trio of memoirs authored by one of the movement's leaders.

Napoli, Donna Jo. *Fish Girl*. Wiesner, David. 2017. 183 pp. Clarion Books. 9780544815124
She's a mermaid girl with a tail who cannot speak and is the main attraction in an aquarium ruled by a supposed Neptune. Her world seems to be controlled by him and limited to the water-filled glass tank until she meets another girl and yearns to explore the world outside; gorgeous illustrations in a story about exploitation.

O'Connor, George. *Artemis: Wild Goddess of the Hunt* (Olympians). 2017. 80 pp. First Second. 9781626725218
Artemis, the goddess of hunting and protector of women and girls, is the heroine of this adventure in a series of graphic novels showcasing Greek mythology.

Stevenson, Noelle. *Nimona*. 2015. 266 pp. HarperTeen. 9780062278234
Lord Ballister Blackheart is a villain, and young Nimona is his sidekick. But their character and power are not as they appear. Packed with humor and a lively and mysterious female lead, the story of good versus evil is not always clear-cut; notable especially for the control of the narrative by those in power and the corrupting influence of that power.

Telgemeier, Raina. *Ghosts*. 2016. 239 pp. Scholastic. 9780545540612
Cat and her family have moved to Northern California where the warm air is easier to breathe for her younger sister afflicted with cystic fibrosis. As the family deals with a life-threatening illness, Cat and Maya learn about the area's missions and cultural traditions.

Wilson, G. Willow. *Ms. Marvel: No Normal*. 2015. 120 pp. Alphona, Adrian. Marvel Worldwide. 9780785190219

Kamala is a young Muslim girl who yearns to party with other kids her age against the wishes of her strict parents. She runs out one night and discovers she has superpowers to help others; disruptive of gender and religious stereotypes.

Yang, Gene Luen. *The Shadow Hero*. Liew, Sonny. 2014. 176 pp. First Second. 9781596436978
Nineteen-year-old Hank is the son of a grocer whose mother has ambitions for him to become a superhero. Following the death of his father, he discovers a spirit power and becomes the Jade Tortoise avenging his father's death. An afterword details the original Green Turtle comic book character.

15

Reframing and Rewriting the Story from Alternate Perspectives (Lesson Plan)

In the scenario in Chapter 14, Jamie had her students look closely at a page in a graphic novel and consider whose perspective is privileged in the telling. An important critical literacy practice is to reconstruct or reframe a narrative from different perspectives. This may involve taking a historical lens to understand characters or events in order to think about how understanding history from another point of view or culture might change our understanding of the story. A basic tenet of critical literacy is that no text is neutral; an author always brings his, her, or their own cultural and social history to the writing of the text. Readers are also empowered to bring their experiences and cultural frameworks to the reading of a text. By questioning the author and reframing the text, a reader can engage critically with the text and understand how both authors and readers shape a text. Reframing essentially asks the reader to think about whose point of view is represented in the text and to consider the text from another point of view. This is particularly powerful when it challenges a dominant point of view and allows another perspective to emerge.

The graphic novel *Ghosts* invites this strategy because of its problematic treatment of a cultural practice, Día de los Muertos, and the history of Spanish missions. In *Ghosts*, Catrina deals with the serious illness of her younger sister who is living with cystic fibrosis. The family has recently moved to Northern California, and Catrina encounters smiling, happy ghosts in a nearby, deserted mission. A large portion of the story features the holiday of Día de los Muertos and Catrina's participation in the event where she also encounters and interacts with ghosts. The book was applauded for its treatment of a family dealing with the serious and life-threatening illness of a child. The author was inspired by the illness and death of a young cousin, and her book received acclaim from the *New York Times* and NPR radio and was recognized with the Eisner Award.

However, almost immediately it was criticized for its appropriation of the holiday of Día de los Muertos as a key element of the story. Critics said it got key facts about the religious observance wrong and the author clearly appropriated a cultural practice for which she had little understanding or experience (Jensen, 2016; Jiménez, 2016; Reese, 2016). In addition, the happy ghosts in this story are encountered in the ruins of a Spanish mission. The purpose and history of these missions to convert native people to Catholicism often in a harsh and violent manner were glossed over as well as the enslavement of native people by the missions. Reese (2016), in particular, questioned whether these ghosts would truly be happy.

Sharing a book such as *Ghosts* that was both widely praised and widely criticized with students in a middle school classroom provides a teachable moment to address these questions. In this lesson, students reframe the author's note to address these criticisms. Like the author of *Ghosts*, students may have naive and uninformed ideas about the native and Latino cultures of the United States, particularly California, and will need to move outside of the book to research and better understand this alternative perspective. Students should also be encouraged to talk about the theme of *Ghosts* and how the author used these problematic elements to address the theme of the acceptance of death. How might the author have reframed several of the scenes in the book? And how could the author have addressed her own position relative to the cultural portrayals in the story?

As this lesson involves looking at professional reviews of a book, conducting research, and citing sources, it is a great lesson to complete in collaboration with the school librarian in the library. The following lesson is framed as one led by the school librarian in the library. The librarian shares book reviews of *Ghosts*, both positive and critical, and asks students to think about the cultural critiques. She also has the students read and discuss the author's note discussing the author's position relative to the topics included in the book. She asks students whether they think the author's research about the observance of Día de los Muertos was sufficient. Was Día de los Muertos part of the author's family or cultural history? The librarian then leads pairs of students in research about aspects of the observance and asks them to compare what they learn with the portrayal of Día de los Muertos in the book *Ghosts*. The librarian leads the students in composing a new "reader's note" that reframes the portrayals in the text with more authentic details.

In this lesson, the critical literacy element of talking back to texts is the focus (Christensen, 2017; Leland, Ociepka, Kuonen, & Bangert, 2018). Readers are actively engaged in questioning the text and the author's appropriation of another culture. Rather than passively accepting the author's portrayal of Día de los Muertos, students conduct research to understand the holiday and its traditions. They are then provided with an opportunity to author a "reader's note" conveying their new understandings.

Table 15.1   Lesson Plan

Central focus: Students will *critique* details in the portrayal of Día de los Muertos in the graphic novel *Ghosts*.	Subject: Language arts
Grade: 6	Classroom context: Whole group

Standards
CCSS.ELA-Literacy.RL.6.2 Determine a theme or central idea of a text and how it is conveyed through particular details; provide a summary of the text distinct from personal opinions or judgments. CCSS.ELA-Literacy.W.6.8 Gather relevant information from multiple print and digital sources; assess the credibility of each source; and quote or paraphrase the data and conclusions of others while avoiding plagiarism and providing basic bibliographic information for sources.
Objectives
Students will *know* how to create a bibliographic citation. Students will *understand* that authors write from a cultural perspective and may not be sensitive to their own portrayals of other cultures. Students will *be able to* critique the accuracy of particular details in a text and graphics.
Assessment: Each pair of students turns in three facts and provides citations to their sources. For each fact, they are expected to find pages in the text of *Ghosts* where these are represented (correctly or not). The librarian assesses their work for completeness: Does each pair have three unique facts with complete and correct citations? Were they able to connect at least two of the facts with the text of *Ghosts*? The librarian leads the class in a shared writing activity to author a new "reader's note" with the facts as recorded in the Google Doc.
Materials
Online materials may be curated by the librarian in a Google Doc where students have access. Online reviews critiquing *Ghosts*:

- http://www.teenlibrariantoolbox.com/2016/07/reading-and-wrestling-with-ghosts-by-raina-telgemeir/
- http://readingwhilewhite.blogspot.com/2016/09/on-ghosts-and-magic-of-day-of-dead.html
- https://americanindiansinchildrensliterature.blogspot.com/search?q=ghosts
- https://booktoss.blog/2016/09/18/ghosts-swing-and-a-hard-miss/

Recommended resources for researching Día de los Muertos:

- https://www.nationalgeographic.com/travel/destinations/north-america/mexico/top-ten-day-of-dead-mexico/
- https://www.inside-mexico.com/category/holidays/dayofthedead/
- http://latino.si.edu/LVM/DayOfTheDead

Online databases as subscribed to
Google Docs for recording research findings/or paper and pencil
Copies of *Ghosts*
Projector and screen
Student devices—one per pair to access the Internet
Copy of Graphic Organizer for Note-Taking (Figure 15.1)

(Continued)

Table 15.1 Lesson Plan (Continued)

Academic language function: Critique	Language demands: Participate in discussion, engage in research, note-taking, and citation; participate in shared writing

Lesson introduction: Students have finished reading the graphic novel *Ghosts* in their language arts classroom and have come to the library to learn about book reviews and conduct research to critique details in the book and write a shared "reader's note" for the book. They come to the library with their copies of the text.

1. The librarian says, "I understand you have just finished reading *Ghosts* by Raina Telgemeier, which won an Eisner Award. But not all critics were happy with the book. Do you have an idea about why?" She waits for responses.

2. The librarian projects several reviews and reads key excerpts. (See the Materials section for URLs to reviews.)

3. The librarian asks students to summarize the criticisms using the think-pair-share strategy. First, students consider the criticisms independently. Next, they share their thinking with a peer. Then, each pair shares their ideas with the whole group.

4. The librarian then has students read what the author said in the note at the end of the book. She asks, "From what perspective was Reina Telgemeier writing this book? Does she share any research she did about Día de los Muertos?" Students should respond that the author only says she went to an observance of the celebration and made sketches for her book.

5. The librarian points out that authors (and illustrators) always create a text from their own social and cultural framework. Readers also bring frames to the reading of the text.

6. The librarian says, "Today we are going to conduct research about Día de los Muertos. Given the criticisms from several reviewers, we might find examples where the author got it wrong. We will then work together to reframe the text in a 'reader's note' about Día de los Muertos."

Instructional input

7. The librarian shares with students that they have been assigned to pairs. Each pair has been assigned to some aspect of Día de los Muertos, such as the origin of the holiday, foods, drink, dates, procession or parade, dance, costume, ofrenda, and common misconceptions.

8. The librarian hands out copies of the graphic organizer (Figure 15.1) to each pair, with their topic written on the top.

9. The librarian models how to create a citation for a website using one of the resources and reminds students that if this is one of their resources, they can use this citation. She says, "I will come around to help you with other citations."

10. The librarian reviews the graphic organizer that has space for as many as six facts. She reminds students that they only need to find two or three facts. She says, "If you find the same fact in your second source, you should record it again because this provides verification for the fact—we found it in more than one resource."

11. The librarian refers to the second column that asks students to see if they can find their fact in the text of *Ghosts*. "Remember you might find an example that is wrong. And you should be looking at the pictures as well as the text."

12. "I have put together links to some resources I found with information about Día de los Muertos for you." The librarian shows students how to access these links. In addition, the librarian might show students a database or online encyclopedia if the school has access to these.

13. The librarian summarizes the task for each pair of students. "You are going to find facts in at least two different sources about your aspect of Día de los Muertos. Don't forget to record the sources for each fact and provide citations to the sources. Once you have two to three facts, you should search *Ghosts* to see how the author portrayed that aspect and record page numbers."

Work session

14. Pairs of students are assigned to research an aspect of the holiday from the following list: origin of the holiday, foods, drink, dates, procession or parade, dance, costume, ofrenda, Caterina, and common misconceptions. They should record two or three facts about that aspect of the holiday on the graphic organizer and record citations to their sources. Each pair should also identify any reference to their assigned aspect within the text of *Ghosts*—in the illustrations or words. Students are instructed to provide page numbers and write a brief sentence about how that aspect is accurately and/or inaccurately portrayed.

15. After students are given ample time to work, pairs take turns sharing what they learned.

16. The librarian leads a discussion about how to write their findings as a "reader's note," suggesting it will be a bulleted list with everyone's findings. The librarian explains that a "reader's note" is meant to inform the reader and provide context for understanding a book. (Note: The following steps of this lesson could be completed in another class period if additional time is needed.)

17. The librarian reviews what students discovered and asks, "What would make a good opening sentence?" For example, the librarian might say, "We have recently read *Ghosts* by Raina Telgemeier and learned about criticisms of her portrayal of Día de los Muertos. Our research found the author got some facts about Día correct, but there were other aspects that she got wrong. We would reframe her portrayal to include the following list." The librarian leads class in writing the opening of the reader's note in a Google Doc.

18. Now, the librarian suggests that every pair write their findings in the document.

19. Once that is completed, the librarian and students review the list and make needed edits to the list of findings included in their collaboratively constructed reader's note.

Lesson closure: The librarian returns to the critique of the book and leads students in a discussion using their findings as evidence about the critiques. Do students believe a note such as the one they have written would be adequate, or should the book be rewritten?

Differentiation: Pairs can be assigned relative to ability levels or students' interests in particular aspects of Día de los Muertos. If there are striving readers in the class, the librarian may show students how to have the websites read aloud to them by the computer. In addition, visual learners may be given written copies of the book reviews read aloud by the librarian in Step 2 of the lesson.

Topic _____ Student name(s)_____

Citation for Source One:

Facts that we learned from Source One:	Can you find this depicted in the text of *Ghosts*? Provide page number.
1.	
2.	
3.	

Citation for Source Two:

Facts that we learned from Source Two:	Can you find this depicted in the text of *Ghosts*? Provide page number.
1.	
2.	
3.	

Figure 15.1   Graphic Organizer for Note-Taking

MODIFYING THE LESSON PLAN

Reframing is a powerful tool, particularly when students are asked to reframe a story based on their own experience. In this lesson, the bloggers and reviewers reframe elements of the story based on their own cultural knowledge and experience. Students are asked to explore that reframing through research of their own. Authoring a "reader's note" offers them a chance to talk back to the author. A smaller lesson could focus entirely on how books are reviewed and comparing and contrasting a variety of reviews of the book. Authors of book reviews and members of awards committees also operate from their own cultural and social frames. The library research in this lesson is a type of jigsaw where each pair of students needs to skim the material to find their assigned aspect of Día de los Muertos. Students are given a small taste of library research, including skimming for needed information, note-taking, and citing sources as a scaffold for later research. The lesson could be modified so that one of the resources is selected, and the teacher leads the whole class to work together to find information about Día de los Muertos that confirms or contrasts the way the celebration is portrayed by the author in *Ghosts*. Given the graphic format of the book, some information is also portrayed visually, and students might be given the option of redrawing some of the frames from the book.

References

Adichie, C. N. (2009, July). *Chimamanda Ngozi Adichie: The danger of a single story* [Video file]. Retrieved from https://www.ted.com/talks/chimamanda_adichie_the_danger_of_a_single_story

Anderson, L. W., Krathwohl, D. R., Airasian, P. W., Cruikshank, K. A., Mayer, R. E., Pintrich, P. R., . . ., & Wittrock, M. C. (2001). *A taxonomy for learning, teaching, and assessing: A revision of Bloom's taxonomy of instructional objectives.* New York, NY: Longman.

Association of Library Services to Children. (2008). Caldecott medal: Terms and Criteria. Retrieved from http://www.ala.org/alsc/awardsgrants/bookmedia/caldecottmedal/caldecottterms/caldecottterms

Baker, D. F. (2007). Musings on diverse worlds. *Horn Book Magazine, 83*: 41–47.

Beck, A. S. (2005). A place for critical literacy. *Journal of Adolescent & Adult Literacy, 48*(5), 392–400.

Beers, K., & Probst, R. E. (2016). *Reading nonfiction: Notice and note, stances, signposts, and strategies.* Portsmouth, NH: Heinemann.

Behrman, E. H. (2006). Teaching about language, power, and text: A review of classroom practices that support critical literacy. *Journal of Adolescent & Adult Literacy, 49*(6), 490–498.

Bintz, W. P., & Shelton, K. S. (2004). Using written conversation in middle school: Lessons from a teacher researcher project. *Journal of Adolescent & Adult Literacy, 47,* 482–507.

Bosma, K., Rule, A. C., & Krueger, K. S. (2013). Social studies content reading about the American Revolution enhanced with graphic novels. *Social Studies Research & Practice, 8*(1), 59–76.

Bowers-Campbell, J. (2011). Take it out of class: Exploring virtual literature circles. *Journal of Adolescent & Adult Literacy, 54*(8), 557–567.

Carano, K. T., & Clabough, J. (2016). Images of struggle: Teaching human rights with graphic novels. *The Social Studies, 107*(1), 14–18.

Christensen, L. (2017). Critical literacy and our students' lives. *Voices from the Middle, 24*(3), 16–19.

Clark, J. S. (2014). Teaching historical agency: Explicitly connecting past and present with graphic novels. *Social Studies Research & Practice, 9*(3), 66–80.

Clark, J. S., & Camicia, S. P. (2014). Fostering preservice teachers' sense of historical agency through the use of non-fiction graphic novels. *Journal of Social Studies Research, 38*(1), 1–13.

Connors, S. P. (2011). Toward a shared vocabulary for visual analysis: An analytic toolkit for deconstructing the visual design of graphic novels. *Journal of Visual Literacy, 31*(1), 71–91.

Connors, S. P. (2012). Altering perspectives: How the implied reader invites us to rethink the difficulty of Graphic Novels. *Clearing House, 85*(1), 33–37.

Creighton, D. C. (1997). Critical literacy in elementary classrooms. *Language Arts, 74*(6), 438–445.

Daniels, H. (2002). *Literature circles: Voice and choice in book clubs and reading groups* (2nd ed.). Portland, ME: Stenhouse Publishers.

DeFrance, N. L., & Fahrenbruck, M. L. (2016). Constructing a plan for text-based discussion. *Journal of Adolescent & Adult Literacy, 59*(5), 575–585.

Dresang, E. T. (1999). *Radical Change: Books for youth in a digital age.* New York, NY: The H. W. Wilson Company.

Eeds, M., & Wells, D. (1989). Grand conversations: An exploration of meaning construction in literature study. *Research in the Teaching of English, 23*(1), 4–29.

Estes, T. H., & Mintz, S. L. (2016). *Instruction: A models approach* (7th ed.). Boston, MA: Pearson.

Fisher, D., & Frey, N. (2014). *Close reading and writing from sources.* Newark, DE: International Reading Association.

Forest, D. E., & Kimmel, S. C. (2016). Critical literacy performances in online literature discussions. *Journal of Education for Library and Information Science, 57*(4), 283–294.

Freire, P. (1970/2012). *Pedagogy of the oppressed.* New York, NY: Continuum.

Freire, P., & Macedo, D. (1987). *Literacy: Reading the word and the world.* South Hadley, MA: Bergin & Garvey Publishers, Inc.

Gall, E., & Gall, P. (2015). Comics are picture books: A (graphic) novel idea. *Horn Book Magazine, 91*(6), 45–50.

Gibson, M. L. (2018). Scaffolding critical questions: Learning to read the world in a middle school civics class in Mexico. *Journal of Adolescent & Adult Literacy, 62*(1), 25–34.

Gómez, S. H. (2017). Six YA titles that epitomize #ownvoices. Retrieved from https://www.slj.com/2017/04/diversity/six-ya-titles-that-epitomize-ownvoices/

Gonzalez, J. (2015, October 15). The big list of class discussion strategies [Blog post]. Retrieved from https://www.cultofpedagogy.com/speaking-listening-techniques/

Grisham, D. L., & Wolsey, T. D. (2006). Recentering the middle school classroom as a vibrant learning community: Students, literacy, and technology intersect. *Journal of Adolescent & Adult Literacy, 49*(8), 648–660. doi:10.1598/JAAL.49.8.2

Hall, L. A., & Piazza, S. V. (2008). Critically reading texts: What students do and how teachers can help. *The Reading Teacher, 62*(1), 32–41.

Hartsfield, D. (2017). "It's pretty and all, but I want it to be realistic": Exploring children's situational interest in nonfiction books. *The Dragon Lode, 35*(2), 8–16.

Hartsfield, D. E., & Maxwell, N. (2018). Differentiating and promoting critical thinking with nonfiction multimodal text sets. In V. Yenika-Agbaw, R. M. Lowery, L. A. Hudock, & P. H. Ricks (Eds.), *Exploring nonfiction literacies: Innovative practices in classrooms* (pp. 75–88, 107–112). Lanham, MD: Rowman & Littlefield.

Janks, H. (2014). Critical literacy's ongoing importance for education. *Journal of Adolescent & Adult Literacy, 57*(5), 349–356.

Jensen, K. (2016). Reading and wrestling with *Ghosts* by Raina Telgemeier. *Teen Librarian Toolbox*. Retrieved from http://www.teenlibrariantoolbox .com/2016/07/reading-and-wrestling-with-ghosts-by-raina-telgemeir/

Jiménez, L. M. (2016, September 18). *Ghosts*: Swing and a hard miss [Blog post]. Retrieved from https://booktoss.blog/2016/09/18/ghosts-swing-and-a-hard-miss/

Jiménez, L. M., & Meyer, C. K. (2016). First impressions matter: Navigating graphic novels utilizing linguistic, visual, and spatial resources. *Journal of Literacy Research, 48*(4), 423–447.

Jocius, R., & Shealy, S. (2017). Critical book clubs: Reimagining literature reading and response. *The Reading Teacher, 71*(6), 691–702.

Jones, S., & Clarke, L. W. (2007). Disconnections: Pushing readers beyond connections and toward the critical. *Pedagogies: An International Journal, 2*(2), 95–11.

Labadie, M., Wetzel, M. M., & Rogers, R. (2012). Opening spaces for critical literacy: Introducing books to young readers. *The Reading Teacher, 66*(2), 117–127.

Larson, L. C. (2009). Reader response meets new literacies: Empowering readers in online learning communities. *The Reading Teacher, 62*(8), 638–648. doi:10.1598/RT.62.8.2

Lee, C. J. (2011). Myths about critical literacy: What teachers need to unlearn. *Journal of Language and Literacy Education, 7*(1), 95–102.

Leland, C., Harste, J., Ociepka, A., Lewison, M., & Vasquez, V. (1999). Exploring critical literacy: You can hear a pin drop. *Language Arts, 77*(1), 70–77.

Leland, C., Ociepka, A., Kuonen, K., & Bangert, S. (2018). Learning to talk back to texts. *Journal of Adolescent & Adult Literacy, 61*(6), 643–652.

Leland, C. H., & Harste, J. C. (2004). Critical literacy: Enlarging the space of the possible. In V. Vasquez, K. A. Egawa, J. C. Harste, & R. D. Thompson (Eds.), *Literacy as social practice: Primary voices K-6* (pp. 129–135). Urbana, IL: National Council of Teachers of English.

Lewison, M., Flint, A. S., & Van Sluys, K. (2002). Taking on critical literacy: The journey of newcomers and novices. *Language Arts, 79*(5), 382–392.

Low, D. E., & Bartow Jacobs, K. (2018). Literature circle roles for discussing graphica in language arts classrooms. *Language Arts, 95*(5), 322–331.

Luke, A., & Woods, A. (2009). Critical literacies in schools: A primer. *Voices from the Middle, 17*(2), 9–18.

McDaniel, C. (2004). Critical literacy: A questioning stance and the possibility for change. *The Reading Teacher, 57*(5), 472–481.

McLaughlin, M., & DeVoogd, G. (2004). Critical literacy as comprehension: Expanding reader response. *Journal of Adolescent & Adult Literacy, 48*(1), 52–62.

Miller, D. (2013). The dazzling world of nonfiction. *Educational Leadership, 71*(3), 22–27.

Moeller, R., & Becnel, K. (2018). Drawing diversity: Representations of race in graphic novels. *School Library Research, 21,* 1–16.

Moeller, R., & Irwin, M. (2012). Seeing the same: A follow-up study on the portrayals of disability in graphic novels read by young adults. *School Library Research, 15,* 1–15.

National Governors Association Center for Best Practices & Council of Chief State School Officers. (2010). *Common Core State Standards for English language arts and literacy in history/social studies, science, and technical subjects.* Washington, DC: Author. Retrieved from http://www.corestandards.org/ela-literacy

Obeso, D. (2014). Science fiction and fantasy 2014: How multicultural is your multiverse? *Publishers Weekly, 261*(40), 24–31.

Oslick, M. E., Robertson, T., & Parks, M. (2018). Creating spaces for critical conversations on issues of social justice. In V. Yenika-Agbaw, R. M. Lowery, & P. H. Ricks (Eds.), *Using nonfiction for civic engagement in classrooms: Critical approaches* (pp. 95–105). Lanham, MD: Rowman & Littlefield.

Powell, R., Cantrell, S. C., & Adams, S. (2001). Saving Black Mountain: The promise of critical literacy in a multicultural democracy. *The Reading Teacher, 54*(8), 772–781.

Reese, D. (2016, September 17). Not recommended: *Ghosts* by Raina Telgemeier [Blog post]. Retrieved from https://americanindiansinchildrensliterature.blogspot.com/2016/09/not-recommended-ghosts-by-raina.html

Rogers, R. (2002). "That's what you're here for, you're suppose to tell us": Teaching and learning critical literacy. *Journal of Adolescent & Adult Literacy, 45*(8), 772–787.

Smith, J. M., & Pole, K. (2018). What's going on in a graphic novel? *The Reading Teacher, 72*(2), 169–177.

Smith, V. (2016). Unmaking the white default. Retrieved from https://www.kirkusreviews.com/features/unmaking-white-default/

Stewart, M., & Young, T. A. (2018). Defining and describing expository literature. In V. Yenika-Agbaw, L. A. Hudock, & R. M. Lowery (Eds.), *Does nonfiction equate truth?: Rethinking disciplinary boundaries through critical literacy* (pp. 11–24). Lanham, MD: Rowman & Littlefield.

Sun, L. (2017). Critical encounters in a middle school English language arts classroom: Using graphic novels to teach critical thinking and reading for peace education. *Multicultural Education, 25*(1), 22–28.

Tomlinson, C. A., & Moon, T. R. (2013). *Assessment and student success in a differentiated classroom.* Alexandria, VA: ASCD.

Wilfong, L. G. (2009). Textmasters: Bringing literature circles to textbook reading across the curriculum. *Journal of Adolescent & Adult Literacy, 53*(2), 164–171.

Williams, S. J. (2014). Fireflies, frogs, and geckoes: Animal characters and cultural identity in emergent children's literature. *New Review of Children's Literature & Librarianship, 20*(2), 100–111.

Young, S. L. B. (2009). Breaking the silence: Critical literacy and social action. *English Journal, 98*(4), 109–115.

Author/Title Index: Recommended Books for Grades 4–8

Subject Index

About the Authors

Danielle E. Hartsfield, PhD, is assistant professor at the University of North Georgia's Dahlonega campus. She teaches children's literature and other courses in the elementary education program and supervises teacher candidates. Her work has been published in journals such as *Teachers College Record*, the *Journal of Teacher Education*, and *Curriculum Inquiry*, and she has presented at conferences hosted by the American Educational Research Association, the National Council of Teachers of English, and the International Literacy Association. She was a member of the Association for Library Service to Children's 2018 Sibert Informational Book Medal committee.

Sue C. Kimmel, PhD, is associate professor at Old Dominion University in Norfolk, Virginia. She teaches children's literature, curriculum, and library science courses. Her work has been published in journals such as *School Library Research*, *Library Quarterly*, and the *Journal of Teacher Education*, and she has presented at conferences hosted by the American Library Association, the Association of Library and Information Science Educators, and the American Educational Research Association. She has been a member of the Association for Library Service to Children's Newbery, Caldecott, and Notable Books for Children committees.

Made in the USA
Middletown, DE
23 November 2021